Dance Teaching Essentials

...porary Dance based in Leeds

Editorial Committee
Ken Bartlett, Foundation for Community Dance
Julie Crofts, Council for Dance Education and Training
Anne Gallacher, Birmingham Royal Ballet
Veronica Jobbins, Laban Centre London and National Dance Teachers' Association
Helen Laws, Dance UK
Judith Palmer, Association of Dance of the African Diaspora
Rachel Rist, Arts Educational School, Tring
Jeanette Siddall, Dance UK
Christopher Thomson, Learning and Access, The Place

Research by Rachel Gibson

Edited by Ian Bramley

Designed by Oblique Design

Printed by Consider This UK

Published by Dance UK

Cover images:

Background image: **Rubicon Dance.** Photo by Tracey Brown.

Top left to right:
Sue Nicholls PDTD teaching Ballet to RAD degree student. Photo by Merlin Hendy.
Choreographers/dancers for *Mission Tour 2001 & 2003*, Robert Hylton and Bawren Tavaziva. Photo by Eric Richmond.
Richard Alston Dance Company. Photo by Chris Nash.
Photo by Elaine Mayson.

Bottom left to right:
Islington Arts Factory. Photo by Kerry Dean.
Rubicon Dance. Photo by Tracey Brown.
Anusha Subramanyam's Bharata Natyam class at the Patidar Samaj. Photo by Vipul Sangoi.

Contents

Department for Culture, Media and Sport
Rt Hon Tessa Jowell MP
Secretary of State

Dance is one of the nation's most popular activities. Whether as participants or audiences, students or professionals, more people than ever are recognising the benefits of dance for pleasure, education, health and creative expression.

This explosion in dance means that there has never been a greater demand for excellent dance teachers. People's involvement with dance may change over time, but quality dance teaching can equip young people for a lifetime of enjoyment - whether as dance professionals, participants or observers.

I welcome *Dance Teaching Essentials* as an important tool for promoting good practices in all areas of dance education. I am confident that it will prove to be an invaluable source of information for professionals, teachers, students and parents.

TESSA JOWELL

"Without the inspiration and encouragement of my early teachers - one, in particular - I would never have become a professional dancer. My teachers helped me to convert my natural enthusiasm and innate joy of movement into a range of skills which carried me through a long, and moderately successful, career. And with their professional performing experience, my teachers provided a bridge between the daily routine of the ballet studio and the heady world of the stage, where my ambitions lay.

Those who can, do - because a teacher showed them how."

Deborah Bull CBE, dancer, writer, broadcaster

Teachers and leaders of dance work in schools, private studios, dance companies, and community settings. The dance opportunities they provide for young people are wide-ranging. They include African, ballet, Bharata Natyam, Caribbean, contemporary, Irish, jazz, Kathak, street, and tap dance techniques, and the development of performance, choreographic and critical skills.

What is *Dance Teaching Essentials*?

This is not a book about *what* to teach. It is a handbook of essential information for teachers of all styles of dance working in all kinds of teaching situations.

Helping young people achieve their potential, deepen their understanding and extend their skills, and sharing with them a passion for dance, is a joyful activity. It is also a responsibility. Relevant knowledge - about how young people learn and grow, and about healthier dance practice - increases continually. There are implications for dance teachers in changing legislation and in the developing expectations of adults with a duty of care for young people. Dance teachers need to be alert to expanding opportunities for young people to engage with dance as an expression of culture, as recreation, as education and as a possible profession.

Dance Teaching Essentials is a collection of key information across these topics and provides a consensus of current opinion about good practice in dance teaching. It is a practical handbook with short sections that can be dipped into, checklists, case studies, useful contacts and suggestions for further reading.

The primary concern is with young people up to the age of 16, although much of the information is relevant to teaching any age group.

Who is it for?

Dance Teaching Essentials is for dance teachers, student teachers and all those involved in providing, teaching and leading dance with young people.

It will also be of interest to parents and young people looking for good quality dance teaching, and to funders, policy-makers, government departments and decision-makers aiming to promote choice and excellence in the provision of dance activities.

Who wrote it?

The Editorial Committee for this book consisted of the Council for Dance Education and Training, Dance UK, the Foundation for Community Dance, the National Dance Teachers' Association and professionals involved in dance company education work and teaching young dancers. In addition, over 20 teachers and other dance professionals provided comments on the draft text. All those who contributed are listed at the end of the book.

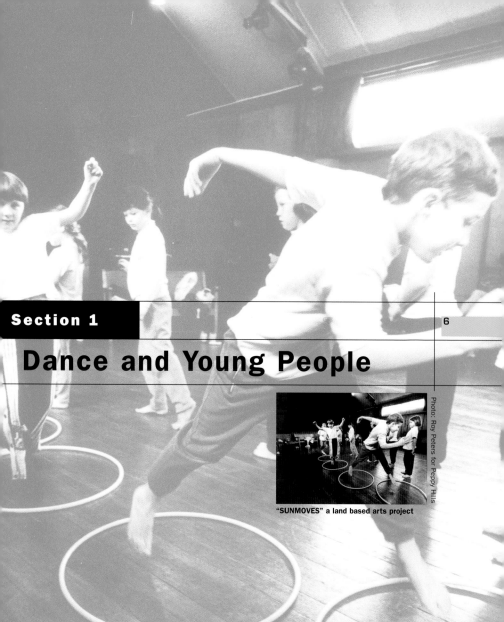

Dance and Young People

Photo: Roy Peters for Peppy Hills

"SUNMOVES" a land based arts project

"I like stretching my muscles and feeling tired afterwards. I enjoy thinking about what I have learned after my ballet class and I try to remember it."

Dayle Innis, participant in Birmingham Royal Ballet's Dance Track programme

Photo: Tracey Brown

Rubicon Dance

Where do children and young people encounter dance?

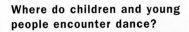

Children and young people encounter dance in school, dance studios, theatres, youth and community centres, dance agencies, carnivals, festivals, on the streets, on television, in pop videos and in advertisements. Dance is an art form in its own right and it interacts with other art forms, so it can be seen in musicals, operas, films and the opening of major sporting events such as the Olympics or Commonwealth Games.

Young people dance for social, recreational, cultural, artistic, educational and vocational purposes – sometimes all at the same time. Dance is taught in primary and secondary schools, where young people may work with professional dance artists as well as their teachers. Beyond school there are opportunities for young people to take graded dance examinations through one of the dance teaching organisations, to create and perform dance as a member of a youth dance group, to join clubs, to participate in workshops and holiday courses, and to dance socially.

There are many ways in which young people encounter dance. But the full range of choices, connections and opportunities to move between dance in school, in the community, in

the private dance studio and elsewhere are not always obvious or explicit. For example, the young person who demonstrates talent for street dancing may need help to connect this with the dance that is on offer in school, or to understand that learning other dance styles can enrich her/his street dance vocabulary.

Opportunities to learn dance

Organisations providing further information are listed in *Resources*

Dance in primary and secondary schools
In state schools all young people experience dance as part of the National Curriculum. In primary schools dance is a compulsory activity in the physical education curriculum and is usually taught by the pupils' classroom teacher. It promotes learning and contributes to cross-curriculum activity. Secondary schools can choose whether to teach dance and it may be taught as part of physical education or performing arts. It is usually taught by Qualified Teacher Status teachers. A number of schools and colleges offer qualifications such as GCSE, AS and A level, BTEC or GNVQ in dance and/or performing arts.

Linda Shipton School of Dancing

Scotland

The Scottish Qualification Authority are presently reviewing and rewriting the National Curriculum Units in the Higher Dance Practice Course. The plan is to divide the Higher Dance Practice Course within the National Curriculum into three units: Intermediate, Higher and Advanced Higher. Students wishing to undertake a Higher Dance Practice Course will be expected to have competence in two of the following dance techniques:
alternative, classical, contemporary, ethnic, jazz or Scottish dance. Practical dance assignments will allow students to develop and apply skills in performance and choreography, plus students will produce a portfolio and written report of work undertaken.

Students in school in the Lothians have the opportunity to link with Telford College of Education, Edinburgh, who facilitate and offer part-time National Curriculum Dance Units. It is hoped this model will develop in Scotland so that schools and colleges can work together in expanding dance provision and training.

Copies of the Units will be available from the Scottish Authority Sales Section (Tel 0141 242 2168; Fax 0141 242 2244), or by contacting:

The Scottish Authority Helpdesk
Hanover House
24 Douglas Street
Glasgow G2 7NQ

Tel 0141 242 2214

The focus for dance in schools is to give young people the opportunity to experience the subject practically while developing an understanding of dance in its broader cultural and social context. It involves young people exploring different ways of moving, developing their own movement vocabulary and creating their own dances. Students develop physical literacy and a critical awareness through talking about each other's dances and studying different dance styles and professional works. Schools with a strong interest in dance offer opportunities to perform, see dance performances and work with professional dance artists.

Dance is also a popular extra-curricular activity. In some schools this enables young people to take further the interest they develop through the curriculum. A range of schemes and initiatives encourage partnerships between schools and with other organisations in order to promote the range and quality of arts education available to young people. Examples include Beacon Schools, Specialist Arts and Sports Colleges, Creative Partnerships and Artsmark.

Further information on dance in schools is available from your local authority.

State education is available to young people throughout the country regardless of their personal circumstances. Other forms of engagement with dance depends, to an extent, on the choice of activity that is available locally, its accessibility and affordability.

Cheshire Dance

Independent dance studios

Approximately 5,000 teachers affiliated to one or more of the teaching organisations work in local, independent dance studios. They reach some 350,000 young people at any point in time. In the main, these studios have no public funding and charge for the classes and examinations that they provide.

Britain is a world leader in providing graded dance examinations. Some of the teaching organisations offer dance examinations worldwide, from the age of four or five. Most offer teaching qualifications and continuing professional development for teachers. Some provide qualified teacher registration.

Graded examinations are taken by 200,000 young people each year in specific dance techniques including ballet, tap, modern, Spanish, and the South Asian dance forms of Kathak and Bharata Natyam. It is estimated that about 75% of students in full-time vocational training have gained graded dance examinations. Graded examinations that meet the relevant criteria are within the National Qualifications Framework, established by the Qualifications and Curriculum Authority to ensure consistency of quality across different awarding bodies.

In general, dance in independent studios involves learning specific dance techniques and styles, taking examinations and taking part in performances, festivals, competitions or displays.

Further information on independent dance studios and dance qualifications is available from the Council for Dance Education and Training.

Music and Dance Scheme

Exceptionally talented young people may be accepted by one of the four specialist boarding schools in England which provide full-time vocational dance training from the age of 11 and offer places through the Department for Education and Skills' Music and Dance Scheme. Competition for these places is tough, and to be successful young people need to demonstrate exceptional talent and physical ability in dance. The allocation of funded places is at the discretion of the school.

Further information on the Music and Dance Scheme is available from the Council for Dance Education and Training or Department for Education and Skills.

Community dance

There are approximately 70,000 opportunities annually for people to participate in local community dance activities. Over half of these are for children and young people. Activities may focus on specific age groups, on young people from particular cultural backgrounds or abilities, or integrate ages, cultures and/or abilities. They are underpinned by a belief that everyone can dance. Activities may be regular and ongoing, or be time-limited special projects. Community dance activities may be provided by professional dance artists, companies and organisations, in partnership with local authorities, the health services and youth, community, and education services.

Linda Shipton School of Dancing

Linda Shipton School of Dancing

A number of community dance initiatives have, over the years, developed into youth dance groups. In 1996 it was estimated there were over 550 youth dance groups across Britain, equivalent to over two per county. Youth dance encompasses a wide range of dance forms including African, ballet, Caribbean, jazz, South Asian and street dance. Some groups specialise in enabling young disabled and non-disabled people to work together.

Youth dance groups usually work towards performances that involve work created by the participants and/or commissioned from professional choreographers. They may also work with musicians, composers and other artists. Larger scale projects might involve several groups working together, performing as part of a dance or arts festival, creating work for film or specific locations. Groups may be run independently, through a dance agency in receipt of local authority or arts funding (see below), or as an extra-curricular school activity. Usually any fees charged are subsidised.

Further information on community dance is available from the Foundation for Community Dance and Community Dance Wales.

Professional company education work
All dance companies in receipt of regular funding from the arts funding system provide education work. Many companies work in schools providing training and support for teachers and occasional workshops or extended projects for students. Some run regular classes for their local communities and schemes for young people aspiring to become dancers. The range of dance forms on offer includes African, ballet, contemporary and South Asian.

Many dance companies have specialist education staff and some companies work exclusively in educational settings. All need to generate some income from their educational activity but it may be subsidised, for example through arts funding, charitable trusts or sponsorship.

Further information is available from individual companies, or though the Arts Council of England, Arts Council of Northern Ireland, Arts Council of Wales or Scottish Arts Council.

Dance Agencies
Dance Agencies often act as brokers between professional dance artists, community groups and schools. They may plan, manage and subsidise projects. They also provide valuable advice and information, manage youth dance groups and offer regular dance activities for young people. Most receive funding from their local authority and the arts funding system, and raise funds from charitable trusts and sponsorship.

In England there is a network of National Dance Agencies and county dance agencies. Scotland has a growing network of dance centres and dance development posts including Dance Base in Edinburgh, the National Centre for Dance, and Citymoves Dancespace in Aberdeen. In Wales there is the Rubicon in Cardiff.

Further information on local community dance activities is available from your local dance agency or country arts council.

Photo: Chris Nash

Richard Alston Dance Company

Taking it further

Young people can take their dance interest further, developing their skills, talent and involvement. This might be through dancing more often, learning different styles or through tackling more complex dance activities. It might include gaining qualifications in specific dance forms, at GCSE, AS and A levels, studying for a degree or teaching qualification, or pursuing a postgraduate degree at MA, MSc, MPhil or PhD level. Dance offers careers for performers and makers of dance, and for teachers, rehearsal directors, administrators, managers, health practitioners, writers and technicians.

Many of the larger dance companies, dance agencies and vocational schools provide advanced programmes for talented young people. Other opportunities for advanced study are offered through special projects and holiday courses. In Scotland there is one specialist boarding school: the Dance School of Scotland in Glasgow (Tel 0141 954 9124).

A number of colleges of further education offer dance courses for post-16 year olds that provide opportunities at entry and higher levels. Some of these courses provide a good foundation for aspiring professional dance artists. It is possible for young people to pursue an interest in dance outside school and move into more formal educational structures post-16.

Dance can be studied at university. Some offer dance as part of a joint honours degree, others as a subject in its own right. Individual courses vary in their emphasis on practical and academic work. Some universities have strong dance departments and offer opportunities for study at postgraduate and research levels.

Young people aiming to become dancers or choreographers will probably go on to full-time training at one of the vocational training institutions, most of which offer three-year courses. Some institutions take students from the age of 16, others from 18, and their courses lead to diploma or degree qualifications. Entry is by audition, and assessment is usually made on dancing ability. Vocational dance schools are accredited by the Council for Dance Education and Training, and further or higher education quality assurance procedures. Students may be eligible for funding by the Department for Education and Skills through the Dance and Drama Awards scheme. Awards to students are allocated by the schools, and may be means tested. A small number of schools are funded through the Higher Education Funding Council and their students are eligible for grants in the same way as young people attending universities.

Currently, aspiring dancers in South Asian and African dance forms and those with disabilities may find their choice of vocational training is limited, although it is likely that opportunities will increase in future years.

Photo: Jason Budge

Vincent Dance Theatre

"I like dancing because it is good fun and physical. I like working creatively as it makes me feel happy"

Cieran Hopkins, participant in Birmingham Royal Ballet's Dance Track programme

Identifying talent

Young people may demonstrate talent in dancing, performing or choreography. Dancing is physically demanding and some forms of dance require a particular kind of physique in order to perform it at the highest level. As children and young people grow, their physique can change significantly and this might make the possibility of a career as, for example a ballet dancer, more difficult and challenging. Early training in one style can still provide a good foundation for dancing in different dance forms and styles.

For an aspiring dancer, wanting to dance is as important as physical qualities. Other useful attributes include determination, expressive qualities and musicality. Performing talent, for example including singing and acting as well as dancing, can lead to a career in musical theatre. Choreographic talent is usually demonstrated at a later age and may not depend on an individual's own physical ability.

Talent can only be identified if young people have opportunities to discover, develop and demonstrate their gifts. The best teachers provide such opportunities and are alert to the range of possible training and career routes.

Dance in the adult world

Dance is enriching. Through dance young people learn about themselves, other people and the world in which they live.

Dance is for life. While an individual's involvement in dance may change over time, quality dance teaching equips young people for a life-time of enjoyment: whether as dance artists, participants or observers. The best teachers help young people make connections. By offering signposts to further opportunities and promoting positive and informed choices, teachers enable young people to develop their relationship with dance as their lives and priorities change.

Dance is a growing art form; there are many more companies today than there were in the 1970s, and audiences for dance are growing faster than for any other art form. Some 15 million people engage with professional dance artists each year, and many more dance for recreation.

Dance is an industry. Careers for dancers are precarious; most dancers have careers that involve a number of different elements and frequently work on short-term contracts. Dance also provides employment for promoters, managers, administrators, accountants, marketing staff, funders, writers, technicians and therapists as well as dancers, teachers and choreographers.

Dance is a collaborative and innovative art form. Dance artists collaborate with artists in music, design, visual art, theatre, opera, film, and dance is part of the entertainment and creative industries. Digital technology is providing new ways of working with dance.

What do young people learn through dance?

Physical health and fitness
- Development of co-ordination, strength, stamina, flexibility and mobility
- Development of physical confidence and control
- Understanding of how the body works and the importance of taking a responsible attitude to maintaining general health and fitness
- Enjoyment in moving

Cultural awareness
- Access to a rich diversity of cultures
- Practical appreciation of different cultures
- Experience of cultural values and traditions
- Understanding of the processes of cultural mobility, fusion and change

Artistic and aesthetic understanding and appreciation
- Understanding of a core artistic discipline
- Access to a unique means of translating ideas, expressing meaning and communicating with others
- Kinaesthetic awareness, physical literacy
- Development of facility in performing, making and appreciating an art form
- Access to collaboration with other art forms
- Understanding of the creative process, developing creative thought and action
- Understanding of artistic products
- Development of observational and perceptual skills, the ability to make informed and critical judgements

Personal and social understanding and skills
- Opportunities to explore the relationship between feelings, values, ideas and expression
- Experience of communicating with others
- Development of confidence and self-esteem through achievement
- Experience of working with other people; opportunities to work as a member of a team and develop leadership skills

- Experience of giving and receiving feedback
- Awareness of career options in dance and other arts

Learning skills
- Learning to learn
- Enhancement of memory through physical patterning and repetition
- Development of verbal and non-verbal communication
- Development of skills in problem-solving
- Opportunities to improve own learning and performance

Literacy
In recent years we have become used to the idea of literacy as much more than just reading and writing. Increasingly we think of ourselves as visually literate; adept at 'reading' the meanings or connotations of advertisements, 'brands', labels and icons. We are also starting to speak of a literacy of the body. It is commonly accepted that we can 'read' emotional states and social attitudes from the mixture of posture, gesture, bodily tension and facial expression that we call body language. In the twenty-first century, being literate in these languages is part of being emotionally and socially mature.

Not surprisingly, dance can make a positive contribution to all these different kinds of literacy. Dance education projects are often explicitly linked with aims in reading and writing. Working in dance involves focusing intensely on communication in and through movement. Dance is so good at working with other art forms that learning about movement in space is readily linked with learning about movement on video or in social contexts, or about form and representation in the visual arts. Through dance people become involved in expression and interpretation, in making meaning in many different ways and in learning to 'read' movement: as emotional expression, as pure form and as narrative.

In Practice

Young Dancers

Young people talk about their experiences of specialist dance training.

Participants in The Royal Ballet's Chance to Dance Programme

I started ballet classes because I was shocked and amazed at how well the Royal Ballet dancers danced and also how they moved to the music. When I was auditioned I felt really nervous, but once I started and got going I thought I was really good and I knew I was good because I got in! When I got in I was so, so and more so excited because you only have one chance. I didn't have to go but I did only go because I enjoyed the stretches and the barre work.

I enjoy everything about my dancing but especially learning new moves and being able to do the moves. It makes me feel good inside and really proud. I also enjoy it because I have the best privilege of being allowed and having permission to go to the Royal Opera House. My most best performance was going to the Royal Opera House and playing the changeling boy. It made me feel all bubbly inside when everyone clapped and it looked like no one was there.

Dancing to me means a lot especially when something new comes up. It really means a lot because I am only here because of my teachers who taught me these things. Dancing is like everything to me, it's a really fun and exciting experience. When I grow older I want to be a ballet dancer - to have fun and so I can communicate and understand ballet more.

Isaac Ezra Lee-Baker, Sudbourne Primary School, London

I started ballet classes because I was impressed by the dancing. At the workshop I was very excited by dancing because it made me feel good. When I was chosen I was very proud. I enjoy learning the different moves and positions. When I visit the Opera House I feel special.

I enjoy all the performances and especially being on stage at the Opera House. The dancing is a very special thing to me. My first performance, *La Fille Mal Gardée,* was very exciting because everybody came to see us. At the end I was a bit shocked at the applause. My dancing is very precious to me.

Lewis Bergin (8), Reay Primary School, London

Broughton High School, Edinburgh

Dancing is all I have ever wanted to do. Since my first ballet class, when I was three, it has always been my dream to be a professional dancer. So when I heard about the project at Broughton I just had to go. I passed the audition and was in.

The teachers were so welcoming and made the class fun. I found the classes easy and very few people had done dance before so I felt a bit bored. But looking back now I realise how much going back to basics helped me. Classes now are challenging, and each day it is a delight to see what exercises have been conjured up to test our ability.

The atmosphere in class is great; all the dancers get on really well with each other and our relationship with our teachers is not purely on a pupil-teacher basis. It's much more than that: they really care about us and it feels like one big family.

We're always working hard for some show or performance. These have taken us all over Edinburgh. We also went to the Millennium Dome, which was the highlight of my time at Broughton.

Dance is not just a job or profession. It can simply be for fun, and the specialist dance unit caters for all kinds of people, whether they have done dance before or not.

Charlotte Fraser

I am now in the fourth year. Prior to staring specialist dance in the first year I hadn't done much dancing, but desperately wanted to be a dancer. The specialist dance course provided me with experience in ballet, contemporary, jazz and tap, and has also given me numerous chances to improve my performance skills.

I have performed in many places including Broughton School's theatre, Telford College, Edinburgh Conference Centre and the Kings' Theatre, but the most memorable was dancing in the Millennium Dome. Dancing in *Our Town Story* in the Millennium Dome was an experience I will never forget. The rehearsals were tiring and we had an amazing time dancing in three full shows.

It might appear that I am only writing about the good aspects of the course, but in my opinion if you are prepared to work hard and try your best then the only bad thing is the nervous feeling you get in the pit of your stomach when receiving your assessment result and before walking on stage.

I have thoroughly enjoyed my three years on the Specialist Dance Course and would definitely do it all over again.

Lauren Vincent

Arts Educational School, Tring

Life at a vocational school differs from a regular school in many ways. One of the biggest differences is that we receive dance training alongside academic studies with an equal amount of time spent on each. Daily vocational classes encourage consistent progress and ensure that we build up the stamina and strength needed to be a professional dancer.

Another important difference is that we have many different dance teachers, not only for each subject, but also within each subject. Being taught by a greater selection of teachers is important as they all teach in slightly different ways. We are able to work with different images and corrections until we find the ones that work best for us. Dancers need to be versatile and to adapt to the way that different choreographers and directors work. We also have classes with guest teachers and workshops where members of a dance company will work with us on a piece of repertoire. This prepares us for employment, as we begin to understand how a member of a company is expected to work, and provides us with contacts within the dance profession.

Performance is a big part of dance training and I have had many chances to perform both repertoire and new pieces choreographed especially for us in a proper theatre. These experiences have taught me about my responsibilities during rehearsals and performances, including ensuring I have done an adequate warm-up and that I am ready to perform.

We benefit from having medical staff and a physiotherapist on site who are able to treat specific dance related problems and injuries quickly, before small problems become complicated injuries. The medical staff give talks on nutrition and injury prevention, which are very important and can be easily overlooked outside the school environment.

One of the biggest advantages of attending a vocational school is that you associate and work with other people who share the same interests and ambitions as you. Healthy competition can develop, but nobody is isolated because they are different and don't fit in.

Melanie Pope

Section 2

Dance Teachers

Photo: Elaine Mayson

"Laura was a really nice teacher, even though she made us work hard she gave us breaks and was supportive. She encouraged us."

Participant in Shobana Jeyasingh Dance Company's Half Term project

Photo: Merlin Hendy

Sue Nicholls PDTD teaching Ballet to RAD degree students

The role of the dance teacher

Dance teachers have a special role in the lives of young people. In addition to developing skills in dance, they influence young people's belief in themselves, their confidence and their understanding of the wider world, their social skills and their aspirations.

The range of dance teaching is enormous. Some people teach dance full-time in schools, studios, community settings or dance companies. Others teach dance alongside other roles as dancers, choreographers, dance development leaders, youth workers, teachers of other subjects, or other jobs.

Knowledge is continually increasing, and dance teachers need to continually learn. They require up-to-date knowledge about, for example, how young people learn and grow, the links between psychological well-being and physical and academic achievement, dance medicine, general health, educational strategies and career options.

Dance teachers are important role models and representatives of dance. The best are open to new ideas and to new opportunities to enrich the dance experience of the young people with whom they work. They continually evaluate their practice, make use of professional support networks and continue their own professional development. They recognise the individuality of every young person, and seek to create an environment and atmosphere that promotes learning, self-esteem and mutual respect.

A changing society

Society expects more and more of people with responsibility for the care, education and development of young people. This can be seen, for example, in the inspection and accountability of all organisations in receipt of public funding, and in the development of a national framework for qualifications. Further information about the legal framework in which dance teachers operate is provided in section 6, *The Legal Framework*.

Britain includes a wealth of cultures, and is increasingly culturally diverse. Within each cultural group there are many sub-groups, distinguished by family and individual histories, beliefs and customs. As a society we are committed to promoting equality of opportunity, and have laws that prohibit discrimination. The Human Rights Act prohibits discrimination "on any ground such as sex, race, colour, language, religion, political or other opinion, national or social origin, association with a national minority, property, birth or other status". Since the introduction of the Disability Discrimination Act in 2001 it is illegal to discriminate against disabled people.

Dance is particularly good at promoting knowledge and understanding of other cultures. Through dance, some of the ways in which cultures are expressed can be clearly seen or experienced through the body. Dance also provides a starting point for learning about the cultural context in which it sits – in other words for becoming genuinely 'culturally literate'.

Our understanding of the possibilities of dance continues to change, reflecting a range of cultural and artistic influences. Artistically, the distinctions between dance forms and between the classical and the contemporary, are being broken by dance artists seeking to create and interpret dance works that are relevant, challenging and meaningful to contemporary audiences.

What qualities do dance teachers need?

An effective and successful teacher of dance:
• has sufficient dance skills, knowledge and understanding to teach the relevant age and ability range
• understands and implements the essential principles of safe practice
• has a passion for teaching and can impart their enthusiasm for dance
• has a clear sense of her/his purpose and values in teaching
• calls on a range of teaching methods and strategies to promote and develop skills in dancing and performing, creativity, understanding and appreciation of dance
• is a good listener, observer and communicator, and is able to engage and develop good relationships with young people
• understands progression routes within and across dance forms
• derives personal enjoyment and satisfaction from enabling people to develop and learn through dance.

An effective and successful teacher of dance is committed to:
• treating young people with dignity, consistency and consideration, valuing and respecting their diverse cultural, religious and ethnic backgrounds, and their experiences and interests
• having high expectations of participants and to realising their potential
• the same positive values, attitudes and behaviour that she/he expects from young people

• communicating sensitively and effectively with parents and carers, respecting their roles, rights and responsibilities
• improving her/his own teaching by continually evaluating her/his practice and participating in continuing professional development.

Continuing professional development

Teachers reflect on their practice and evaluate it in order to improve the effectiveness of what they do. A self-evaluation checklist is included in *Resources*. Asking students for feedback on classes, workshops and projects reinforces their learning and contributes to the teacher's self-evaluation.

Opportunities for professional development are provided by the teaching organisations that provide graded examinations, qualification awarding bodies, dance agencies and companies, and in-service training programmes in schools and educational institutions.

Teachers employed by organisations may find it easier to undertake professional development; it may be required and/or rewarded by their employer. Self-employed and freelance teachers need to take responsibility for their own professional development, and be proactive about seeking opportunities and finding the necessary time and financial resources. Joining relevant organisations and subscribing to publications are good ways of remaining informed. Attending courses, conferences and events has the additional benefit of providing opportunities to meet and talk with colleagues.

Professional development for dance teachers can include keeping up to date with syllabuses and examination procedures, developments in education, healthier dance practice, dance science, training and career opportunities, and dance performances.

Photo: Hanson

David Nixon, Artistic Director, Northern Ballet Theatre

Photo: Merlin Hendy

Rhian Robbins LRAD, Dip LCDS teaching children from Ravenstone Primary School.

Dance teaching qualifications

There are different kinds of dance teaching qualifications required by different teaching situations. It is essential that dance teachers receive appropriate training and qualifications from recognised institutions.

Teaching in state schools

Applicants for teaching posts of virtually any subject in all maintained (state) and direct grant schools must hold Qualified Teacher Status (QTS), which is awarded by the Department for Education and Skills (DfES) through the Teacher Training Agency (TTA).

At present, only teachers with QTS are allowed to teach dance in state schools as a permanent member of staff. Guest artists may be invited to teach classes or workshops providing that a QTS teacher is present.

QTS is a degree level qualification. This can be achieved through a Bachelor of Education degree, or a Bachelor of the Arts (BA) or Bachelor of Science (BSc) degree with QTS. Anyone with a degree recognised by the DfES can go on to study for a Post Graduate Certificate of Education (PGCE). Contacts for information on Initial Teacher Training are included in Further Information in *Resources*.

Teaching in the private sector

Teachers working in the private sector are usually self-employed, and may be based at leisure centres or local dance schools. Private dance teachers usually work through one of the dance teaching organisations. These organisations offer a range of examinations for children and young people as well as teacher training programmes which lead to the organisation's own teaching diplomas and certificates. Some teaching organisations maintain a Register of Teachers and only teachers registered with the organisation may enter children and students for examinations.

A list of teaching organisations is included in Further Information in *Resources*.

There are also opportunities for teaching dance overseas. Contact the relevant embassy for information on professional qualifications and teaching requirements in that country.

Teaching in the community

Community dance practitioners have often completed vocational training or degrees in dance. In addition, there are a number of courses in community dance leading to degree or diploma qualifications. Shorter and part-time courses include Dance Leaders in the Community offered by some colleges, dance centres and agencies, and the Laban Guild's Community Dance Teachers course.

Qualifications are more varied in community dance. Contact the Foundation for Community Dance or Community Dance Wales for further information.

In Practice

Schools and Studios

Developing dance in a primary school, in a secondary school and in an independent dance studio.

Sextons Manor Community Primary School, Suffolk

Dance at Sextons Manor begins as soon as children enter the nursery. Taught as part of the PE curriculum, dance is an integral part of the school's Christmas performances and leavers assemblies, and a number of after-school dance clubs run throughout the year. The Suffolk PE and Sport Advisory Team has produced a long-term plan for PE which the school has chosen to use. As dance co-ordinator at the school I am compiling sequences of lessons to cover the dance learning objectives.

As with all curriculum subjects, time is precious. With this in mind, I try to link dance to other curriculum subjects. For example, some sequences of lessons are based on stories and linked to literacy; others are linked to a science topic such as 'Ourselves', where the inspiration for movement comes from exploring ways of moving different parts of the body. Sequences of dance lessons have clear dance objectives. There are opportunities for pupils to compose, perform and appreciate dance. Pupils may improvise or be taught a movement sequence. They are encouraged to build on movements by exploring different actions, dynamics, body parts and ways to travel, jump or turn. As well as dancing individually, children compose and perform with partners and in groups.

Weekly assemblies provide excellent opportunities for pupils to perform to the whole school. There are also opportunities for children to appreciate dance – time to watch others' movements and comment on what they see, to watch a dance video, talk about it and discover ideas for their own movement projects.

Dance is enormously beneficial. It is fun and enables pupils to be creative, to express themselves, and it contributes to their health and fitness. It also raises their self-esteem, particularly when they realise what they have achieved and that other people enjoy watching them dance.

Clare Buxton, Dance Co-ordinator

The Linda Shipton School of Dancing, Ipswich

Linda began teaching in Ipswich 25 years ago. Her studio is attended by approximately 250 children of all ages and levels, studying a variety of disciplines that include ballet, modern, tap and jazz.

All students have the option to take graded examinations and past students have gone on to the Royal Ballet School, Central School of Ballet, Northern Ballet School, Rambert School, Laine Theatre Arts, Bird College, London Studio Centre and Arts Educational School. Classes also incorporate non-syllabus work to involve and encourage students that choose not to enter examinations. Drama workshops, taught by a local drama teacher, have also been introduced. The school is heavily involved in the local community: students participate in charity events, local dance festivals, pantomime and summer shows.

Linda attends and organises local teachers' courses on various topics, including syllabus updates, first aid and child development. She helped to found the Suffolk Ballet Scholarship Scheme, which provides subsidised weekly lessons for talented children, enabling them to be taught by highly experienced teachers and helping them to discover whether they might want to pursue ballet professionally.

"I enjoy seeing pupils develop both personally and 'dance-wise'. Even if they do not go on to a dance career, I find the confidence they develop most satisfying. Nowadays it is also lovely to teach the children of past students. It is super to see ex-students become soloists in The Royal Ballet and English National Ballet, perform in the West End, on TV and cruises, or become teachers in various parts of the world. Equally, it is most touching when a child doesn't want to go home after their lesson because they love their dancing so much!"

Linda Shipton, *Principal*

The Lindsey School Community Arts College, Cleethorpes

The Lindsey School (TLS) Community Arts College is a mixed ability 11-18 school with over 1,500 students, many of whom enter the school with below average standards of attainment. Parents frequently cite our track record in the performing arts as a reason for choosing the school, and we are oversubscribed by about 20%.

Dance arrived at TLS in 1992 and GCSE dance was introduced in 1993. Now 110 students are studying dance in Key Stage 4 and all students study dance in Key Stage 3. Students can take dance units within GCSE Expressive Arts, GNVQ Performing Arts and at A level. The school achieved Arts Status in November 1999 and in 2001 we achieved Arts Mark Gold.

The Units of Work are progressive and developmental. For each year in Key Stage 3, they include:
- two units linked to professional dance works
- one unit following a cultural strand
- one unit developing contact improvisation and lift work
- one unit with a cross-curricular stimulus
- one free composition unit which builds into the school's Arts Festival.

Some groups can also take a media studies dance unit. We have recently purchased the computer programme, Lifeforms, and aim to provide a technology project for Year 9.

Extra-curricular provision includes lower and upper school dance clubs, and the Grimsby and Cleethorpes Youth Dance Theatre. Increased staffing has improved opportunities for gifted students and boys, and the school participates in Rock Challenge involving around 100 students each year. The Grimsby and Cleethorpes Youth Dance Theatre has performed in the BT Dance Festival, Laban Centre London's Youth Dance Platform and an inter-schools dance performance at the Grimsby Auditorium. We hold an annual dance performance and collaborate with drama, music, art and media studies on other school productions and festivals. In October 2000, the dance teachers from TLS and Community Arts College led two regional choreographic groups in creating and presenting the *Our Town Story* Millennium Dome performance.

Working with professional artists is critical. We have worked with Scottish Ballet, Rambert Dance Company, Motionhouse, Ludus Dance Company, Phoenix Dance Company, Union Dance Company, The Cholmondeleys and The Featherstonehaughs, RJC, Retina Dance Company and Random Dance Company. We also provide dance performances for the local area as there is no small-scale theatre in North East Lincolnshire. The school also provides community dance classes, including pilates and yoga.

Owing to its vision and passion for the arts, The Lindsey School Community Arts College is a vibrant and innovative place. Designation as an Arts Status school has enriched opportunities for a wide cross section of the community and we support neighbouring schools in developing their dance provision. A recent independent audit found us to be a centre of excellence for dance. Dance thrives in this arts-friendly environment; it also plays a key role in promoting other art forms and in the attainment of our students. It is wonderful to feel so proud of our achievements and to have the confidence to go out and share our experience with the wider community.

Stacie Hooks, Head of Dance

Section 3

Teaching and Learning Dance

The Lindsey School Community Arts College

Photo: Stacie Hooks

Dance teaching: where we are and how we got here

French, Russian Courts
16th to 19th centuries
Classical Ballet

Diaghilev 1909-1930
Paris, London
Rambert, De Valois
training, schools,
companies
1950s The Royal Ballet

Education 1900 - fitness
training, Swedish,
Dartmouth College
1940s - Laban analysis,
education methods -
modern educational dance
1990s National Curriculum
(PE), GCSE, A, AS level

USA, 1930s,
Graham, Cunningham,
narrative and abstract
art, political,
contemporary

Britain, 1940s
African, Caribbean,
South Asian
traditional,
classical, jazz,
contemporary

Germany, Europe,
1930s Laban,
Wigman, Jooss,
Expressionist,
theatre, education,
community, therapy

Graded examinations
RAD (1920), ISTD,
IDTA, BBO, etc
Framework extended to
other theatre forms
(tap, modern,
revised Greek)

Britain 1940s/50s - Jooss touring,
Laban teaching, Graham and other
US companies
1960s/70s - influences meld:
The Place (Robert Cohan, Graham Dancer),
Laban Centre London (Bonnie Bird,
Graham Dancer),
Home-grown experiments, including
ballet dancers - British
Contemporary Dance
Today - also includes South Asian,
African, Caribbean, Irish, jazz, street,
physical theatre, disability

1960s - animateurs,
community dance
links between
professional/
educational, creative,
community
development,
youth dance groups
National Dance
Agencies, regional,
county, local agencies

Vocational training - ballet/contemporary, vocational/degree
Education - further and higher education qualifications
Recreation - participant, audience
Work - dancer, teacher, choreographer, manager, community dance practitioner, leader

"I like dancing and becoming more supple as it helps with athletics and all round sports and gymnastics. I really like breakdancing movements as I can do them well."

Adam Brown, participant in Birmingham Royal Ballet's Dance Track programme

Complete and comprehensive dance learning incorporates and integrates dancing and performing, creating and appreciating. This section describes in outline what each of these activities involves.

Photo: Jason Budge

Vincent Dance Theatre

Photo: Tom Martin

Dance 4

Dancing and performing

The fundamentals of dancing consist of discovering a wider range of ways of moving, increasing strength, physical facility and confidence, and enhanced understanding of the possible relationships with space, time and other people.

Technical skills:
• Posture, alignment, flow of energy, co-ordination, balance, strength, flexibility, control and mobility
• Body actions: combinations of flexion, extension, rotation, locomotion, turning, gesture, elevation and stillness
• Dynamics: combinations of speed, energy and continuity, and using contrast, variation and development of these to give accent, rhythm and phrasing
• Space: shaping and orientation of the body in space; size, level, direction and pathways
• Relationships: body part to body part, movement to movement, person to person, inter-action between and sensitivity to other dancers and the space

Expressive skills:
• Focus
• Projection
• Sense of style
• Musicality
• Communication of choreographic intention

• Demonstrating meaning and symbolic significance of movements

There are different approaches to developing technical and expressive skills in dancing. They can be characterised as:
Learning a defined technique such as African, ballet, Bharata Natyam, Caribbean, contemporary, hip-hop, jazz, jive, Kathak, street, tap, ballroom, folk and historical dances. The emphasis is on developing a movement vocabulary through the progressive learning of steps, movements and gestures, movement sequences, and characteristics of style.
Learning through exploration. The emphasis is on responding to tasks and/or imagery, solving problems, improvising and creating dances, and thereby developing movement vocabulary, and physical and expressive skills.

Teachers may specialise in one or other approach, or a mixture of the two. Commonly, students begin by learning simple movements and combinations, and progress to more physically demanding movements and increasingly complex sequences of movement and ideas. They will dance alone, with partners and in groups. Good teaching practice makes use of a variety of strategies for developing skill and understanding, and encourages students to reflect on and articulate their learning.

Photo: Jason Budge

Vincent Dance Theatre

Photo: Kerry Dean

Classes at Islington Arts Factory

Creating dance

Creating dances enables young people to explore and express their own ideas and feelings. Discovering different ways of making dances, the processes of choreographing, improvising, inventing, structuring, shaping and refining - and the power of communicating through dance - enhance artistic, aesthetic and cultural understanding.

Creating dance develops:
- skills in improvising and structuring
- understanding of the craft of choreography and the potential of dance as a tool for expression and communication
- problem-solving skills, the ability to work with others, intuition, reflection, planning, refining
- understanding of creative processes
- appreciation of dance works.

The craft of choreography includes:
- exploring dance ideas in response to various resource material, such as kinaesthesia, text, visual art, music, sound, space, issues, repertoire, styles and traditions
- investigating the potential of dance ideas through creating short sequences, solos and group dances, discussion, researching further resource material
- improvising and making judgements about the selection of movement material that best suits the initial idea, style and individual's perspective
- structuring material, reflecting and improving the material, layering and developing the material through the use of choreographic devices, dynamics, space, relationships
- understanding relationships with sound, music, voice, words, silence
- understanding relationships with design: set, lighting, props, costume, space, video, film, technology
- appraising and evaluating throughout the dance making process
- presenting the dance to others
- evaluating the completed work in the context of the initial idea and the overall effectiveness of the work.

Creativity in dance is fostered by:
- a supportive and safe environment in which inventiveness and experimentation is encouraged and valued
- providing different kinds of tasks, starting points, problems, structures, contexts and objectives
- offering strategies for thinking about connections and different ways of solving problems
- encouraging imaginative responses, spontaneity, reflection, risk-taking and different ways of doing things
- challenging assumptions and initial responses
- giving value to the creative process
- recognising completed dance works and the validity of diverse solutions to creative problems
- language that evokes images and elicits imaginative responses
- reflection, discussion, feedback, evaluation, validation.

Appreciating dance

Dance draws out intellectual, emotional and kinaesthetic responses in the viewer. It inspires, moves and challenges. Through experiencing dance, young people discover more about their responses and understand their achievements, interests and concerns in a wider context. Access to the diversity of dance works, their historical and cultural contexts, and the development of observational and critical skills are essential to learning and appreciating dance.

Photo: Lara Platman

Courtesy of Laban

Watching dance

Appreciating dance also provides the opportunity to develop 'choreographic literacy' – to increase the sophistication with which sequences of movement are watched, read and understood.

New forms of dance expression come into being all the time - including collaborations with other art forms, and forms such as video dance and dance in digital media - and these continually extend understanding of what dance and the aesthetics of dance are.

Education in dance is therefore likely to develop an increasing level of choreographic literacy. This should mean that young people get steadily better at watching dance receptively but critically (in the best sense); being able to appreciate what they are seeing and at the same time be discriminating. Choreographically literate viewers have different ways of watching, depending on the style or form of the dance, and can form opinions and judgements and give reasons to back them up. In this way viewers learn to engage in dialogue with others, and can take part in discussions about the art form and its development.

Watching dance provides opportunities to:

- develop skills in observation, through experiences in class and at performances, and ways of using the information to improve the student's own performance
- understand and connect with social, cultural, historical and artistic contexts for dance
- develop analytical skills
- develop physical literacy
- articulate and discuss dance, to develop a vocabulary for talking about dance
- be inspired - watching can be a stimulus for creating, gaining understanding about performing and motivation to dance more and/or achieve more in dance
- understand the context for students' own dance practice
- understand collaboration across and between art forms.

The meaning and significance of dances is better understood through the process of description, analysis, interpretation and evaluation, giving consideration to the aspects identified under *Creating dance.*

Photo: Josie Bourne

James Brindley Hospital School

Ballybeen Youth Club Boys, Belfast, Men in Black. L to R: David Brown, Thomas Carroll, Aaron Cathcart, Craig McClune and David Nelson

The historical and social context of dances might include:

- purpose, intention in their historical and social context
- distinctive features of the style
- influences of other dance and/or art forms
- dancers, choreographers and other artists.

Some questions to prompt discussion about dance works are provided in *Resources*.

Talking dance

It is vital for the future of dance that dance artists are clear and articulate about what they do and why they do it. They need to be able to contribute to the development of dance through critical debate and discussion with their peers in dance and in other art forms. They need to act as advocates for dance in a wide range of contexts and to a variety of audiences.

Dancers are now expected to contribute to the creative process; to bring other skills to the stage, including dealing with text and voice skills; to manage their own affairs; to be entrepreneurial in creating work opportunities

and in generating income. Language skills are important in all these areas.

Learning to give and take constructive feedback is an important skill in teaching and learning dance, and is applicable in all aspects of life.

Reflecting, articulating and discussing deepen understanding and appreciation. Talking makes watching dance a social experience, it affirms enjoyment, challenges assumptions and broadens understanding of possible interpretations. It also promotes learning. It has value in the contexts of dancing, creating and appreciating, and promotes the integration of the learning that takes place in each of these contexts.

"The very best dancers are extremely intelligent. We need to get rid of this idea that you dance without thinking."

Matz Skoog, *Artistic Director, English National Ballet*

In Practice

Choreographic Projects

Artists reflect on choreographic projects.

Café Atlantic: Birmingham Royal Ballet and Chicago's Gallery 37

Young people in Birmingham and Chicago used web-based resources on David Bintley's Ballet *'Still Life' at the Penguin Café* as a starting point for work with professional dancers. The project culminated in a live performance shared across the Atlantic, with scenes from each city projected live onto giant screens. The result was a single, coherent piece of dance, with a finale in which both cities danced together.

The Birmingham group included a company of disabled and non-disabled dancers from Queensbridge and Fox Hollies Performing Arts College. Queensbridge School is an inner-city secondary for 11-16 year olds, and Fox Hollies School caters for young people with learning difficulties aged from 11-19. They were jointly designated a performing arts college in 2000. Birmingham Royal Ballet has a long-standing relationship with both schools, but this was the first time we had worked with an integrated group of their students.

The process began with 'taster' sessions in two the schools. These introduced the ideas and themes from *'Still Life' at the Penguin Café* so that the participants could input to the selection of a starting point for their piece. These sessions were held separately to gauge each group's needs and abilities and their responses to different ways of working. The knowledge gained in the taster sessions was fundamental to the way in which the integrated sessions were designed, and provided information on which the composer and myself (choreographer) could make certain practical and creative decisions. Working with the groups separately also gave an opportunity to discuss issues of integration, explore expectations and address any concerns before the integrated work began.

Movement ideas were explored, shared and the piece was developed using material based on the young people's ideas. I needed to ensure that everyone was challenged creatively and physically, and that the inclusive approach went beyond the 'social' level. The musical complexity helped introduce a higher level of challenge, for example in floor patterns, jumps and turns. Gradually the emphasis shifted from providing an improvisational framework to a more directed approach, as we set about producing a polished eight-minute performance in only seven, two-hour sessions!

The project presented many new and exciting challenges for all involved. I believe it was largely successful. Perhaps one of the most important contributory factors was the close collaboration between schools, staff and pupils, BRB, composer and choreographer. Flexibility in approach, willingness to share ideas and enthusiasm were key, and resulted in extensive levels of support to and from all participants.

Lee Fisher, Birmingham Royal Ballet Soloist

Sword Dance at Woodlands Junior School, Cheshire

Sanchari Dance Company's residency at Woodlands Junior School in Cheshire, involved two dancers, Bisakha Sarker and Sanjeevini Dutta, musician-composer Nick Wiltshire and visual artist Noelle Williamson, in a five-day residency leading to an after-school performance.

Much traditional South Asian dance involves images based on the rituals of worship and rural pursuits such as collecting water from the well. These might not mean much to pupils in a Cheshire primary school, so we turned to the Indian martial art of Kalari for inspiration. Strong, broad movements, which highlighted body lines and relied less on fine coordination, fired the imagination of the young people. The aspects of inner strength and self-discipline were emphasised, and pupils were able to find the connections between yoga, martial arts and dance. Hanging the non-narrative Sword Dance within the framework of a story, in this case the Indian epic the *Mahabharata*, gave another dimension to the learning experience.

The residency included workshops in music, rhythm and dance. The performance piece combined formal taught sequences with pupils' own movements. This gave it a dynamic and unexpected quality, and pupils had a strong sense of ownership of the dance. On the performance night, dressed in T shirts and shorts with just a scarf for a headband hinting at the martial origins of the dance, the pupils gave an impressive performance. The movements had clarity and were performed with conviction that demonstrated that the pupils had made it their own.

Sanjeevini Dutta, Director, Kadam

CAN DANCE: James Brindley Hospital School, Birmingham

CAN DANCE is a collaboration between two professional dance artists, Peppy Hills and Louise Glynn, and the James Brindley Hospital School in Birmingham. It aims to create high quality dance experiences at a poignant and often life-changing time for the young people and their families. Students come from a variety of social, cultural and ethnic backgrounds, and have a range of physical and psychological illnesses. Dancing in bed whilst connected to hi-tech medical equipment, choreographing and preparing for a performance with live music, or watching and then dancing with a professional touring dance company, are all features of the project.

The main challenge of the work is the need to respond instinctively to a vast array of needs and co-create dance work that is fun, creative and of a high quality. In a fast changing and unpredictable environment, elements such as medication, changes in health, and x-ray and physiotherapy appointments can interrupt the flow of sessions and change what is possible.

Tasks need to be open and differentiated so that students attached to medical equipment or with minimal movement can take part and achieve their maximum dance potential at that point in time. We need to be flexible, start from what is possible and look for the dance potential in every situation: a ward, a patient's belongings, toys or books can all be used as a stimulus or an idea that can be translated into dance. We need to lead but never take over, control or over-ride students' input.

Sessions often involve families - siblings, parents and grandparents - and change the roles of patient/visitor. For example, a 12-year-old girl had to lie flat on her back constantly. We explored the movement possibilities of arms and hands. She selected the movements she liked and, as well as dancing, she choreographed her mother, grandmother and the dance artist. She created a short dance piece that centred around her bed, including changes of level and movements away, underneath and around it. Physically, she was the least able, but she was the decision maker and controlled the piece, as well as dancing in it. It was significant, that at a time in her life where virtually everything had to be done for her, she was able to experience control and decision making through dance.

The dance sessions are challenging, but offer both the scope and stimulus for exciting dance work. For the students, the most vital aspect of the work is that gives them space and the status of dancers and creators.

Peppy Hills, Lead Dance Artist & Project Manager
Louise Glynn, Lead Dance Artist
Sue Cowley, Deputy Head Teacher, James Brindley Hospital School

CastleScape Project: East London Dance and Random Dance Company

CastleScape, was a dance performance by Random Dance Company commissioned by East London Dance as part of the A13 Artscape project and in partnership with the London Borough of Barking and Dagenham and its Department of Education, Arts and Libraries. The Company worked with 60 young people from the Goresbrook Residents Association, and local schools and colleges. The groups created movement material based on an exploration of Random's movement aesthetic and ideas of identity drawn from the local community. The project included an intensive two weeks of rehearsals and culminated with three exciting evenings of original multi-media dance performances in a specially constructed dome on Castle Green, on the Goresbrook Village Estate adjacent to the A13 trunk road.

The central theme was negotiated with participants to ensure their sense of ownership. Sessions building the movement material for the performance involved high energy sequences, moving through space, spatial and numerical tasks. The audience was in the round, and people could roam around the space. This created a relaxed, accessible atmosphere quite unlike a conventional performance.

The project involved creating a dance work for a public environment. Security for equipment and participants meant a perimeter fence had to be erected and a security firm employed. Working with such a large group, in the midst of a residential area and in an unusual performance space, meant that communication was very important, and had to be everyone's responsibility.

The impact on the participants was evident in their enthusiasm and increased self-esteem. The project led to the establishment of a dance group on the Goresbrook estate, an after school club in a local primary school and a further group for young people over the age of 11.

Alex Kenyon, East London Dance Projects Co-ordinator

Section 4

Safe Practice

Rubicon Dance

Photo: Tracey Brown

"I enjoy skipping and doing the splits. When I am dancing it makes me feel special. It makes me feel excited but sometimes nervous because you are performing in front of lots of people. I would be sad if I couldn't do ballet."

Laela Henley-Rowe, *Royal Ballet Chance to Dance participant*

RAD degree student, Gwen Hallam

Photo: Merlin Hendy

Safe practice in dance teaching means that the activity is appropriate to the space, to the physique, age, maturity and gender of the individuals in the group.

Teachers need to be proactive in taking the necessary steps to minimise the risks of harm or damage to students. (Refer also to *Resources*).

The first step is to maintain up-to-date knowledge - about changes in legal requirements and about how young people grow, develop and learn as much as about changes in a syllabus or curriculum.

Physical safety is the most obvious concern. The space should be appropriate for dance. Where this is not possible, then the dance activity must be appropriate to the space. Activity should also be appropriate to the physical and intellectual development of the individuals in the group.

Intellectual and emotional well-being are increasingly recognised as being as important as physical safety. At the most extreme, abuse and bullying are legal offences. Safe practice in this context involves teachers' behaviour and the language that they use. They should ensure that their behaviour and language cannot be considered abusive, and aim to encourage a positive, supportive and mutually respectful working atmosphere. It may be useful to consider teaching/learning contracts, codes of conduct and customer charters that make mutual responsibilities and expectations explicit.

The following checklists provide an overview of safe, and effective, dance practice.

Spaces

Space that is suitable for teaching and learning dance:
- is warm (the Equity minimum recommended temperature is 18°C, but warmer is better)
- is well ventilated
- is well-lit
- has a sprung floor: if this is not possible, then a wooden floor with some 'give' in it
- has a clean floor surface that is not highly polished or slippery
- is without obstacles that will restrict participants' movement or could cause injury if a student collides with them
- has a ceiling sufficiently high so as not to restrict participants' movements.

Spaces should also be accessible for wheelchair users and have adequate and separate toilet and changing facilities for male and female participants. Access to fire exits must not be restricted. There should be sufficient space for musicians and the safe use of any equipment as required.

It is not always possible to work in the ideal environment. In such cases, the activity needs to be designed to be safe for the space, for example:
- If the space is cold, initial activities will ensure participants are well warmed up and students may be encouraged to wear layers of clothing that can discarded as they become warmer.
- If the space is stuffy, there will be frequent changes of activity to help participants maintain their attention.
- If the floor is concrete, jumps and activities that involve falling to the floor will be minimised or avoided.
- If the floor is slippery or dirty, appropriate footwear will be worn. Water or resin might be used to reduce the danger of footwear slipping.
- If the floor is cold or dirty, participants will not be expected to spend long periods of time working on the floor.
- If the space is small, participants might work in smaller groups with those watching being encouraged to offer feedback to those doing.

People

General
- Maintain knowledge of anatomy and physiology in relation to dance activity.
- Appreciate students' individuality, their differing physical abilities and personalities.
- Understand the need to build on strengths, rather than impose one rule on all.
- Promote self-esteem, assertiveness and confidence.
- Understand the benefits of reflection, discussion and evaluation.
- Encourage intellectual understanding in relation to the development of physical facility.
- Ensure appropriate clothing and footwear are worn.

Children and young people
- Understand how a child develops physically, emotionally and psychologically, and the key milestones in child development.
- Be aware of types of exercises that are suitable for particular stages in a child's development.
- Be aware of common childhood ailments, their symptoms and when specialist advice should be sought.
- Be aware of the physical and hormonal changes that take place during puberty and their implications for progress in dance performance.
- Be aware of the physical and related psychological changes that occur during the adolescent growth spurt and understand why certain exercises may need to be adapted, avoided or emphasised at this time.
- Be aware of the significance of body image and the searching for identity at this stage of development, and the implications for psychological well-being and changes in behaviour.

General health, nutrition, hydration
- Understand nutrition and hydration requirements for general health and to provide enough energy for the level of exercise being undertaken by students.
- Ensure students have access to water and recognise the importance of keeping hydrated before, during and after exercise.
- Promote a responsible attitude to general health issues.
- Understand the need to support students emotionally and with sensitivity if they are injured, or suspected of having an eating disorder or other health problem.
- Where appropriate, schools may have written policies defining their approach to support, confidentiality and possible action in case of injury and health problems.

Courtesy of Laban

Photo: Lara Platman

Warm up/cool down

- Understand the importance of adequate warm up/cool down before and after exercise, of allowing sufficient time, and the components that make up an effective warm up/cool down.
- Understand the psychological benefits of warm up/cool down.
- Understand the need to incorporate this into the class structure for younger students, and to ensure older students incorporate warm up/cool down into their dance activities.

Injury prevention

- Ensure the space is appropriate and/or design activity that is appropriate to the space.
- Manage the participants in the space to minimise the risk of accidents.
- Ensure activity is appropriate to the developmental stage of the individuals and the group.
- Be aware of common dance injuries and their possible causes.
- Understand the principles of safe exercise practice associated with alignment, impact and control.
- Be aware of the need for particular care to prevent injury to the neck and spine.
- Encourage older students to take responsibility for their physical safety by warming up, behaving responsibly towards other people, and keeping teachers informed of health and other problems that might affect their performance.
- Encourage students to maintain a healthy life-style.

First aid, injuries and accidents

- Be prepared for injury, accidents or the emergence of general health issues, and know how to deal with such incidents appropriately.
- Know where the nearest telephone is situated.

- Understand any fire and emergency procedures required by the venue.
- Know about reporting procedures for accidents required by the venue.
- Make written reports of any accidents or incidents that result in injury.
- Complete a first aid course, and/or maintain knowledge of basic first aid and when an injury needs to be referred to a medical practitioner or casualty.
- Maintain contact details for parents/carers and local practitioners with experience of treating dancers.
- Maintain a first aid box with appropriate content.
- Do not give medication to students.

Behaviour and language

- Develop open, trusting relationships with students.
- Facilitate communication with students that is two-way.
- Maintain professional, respectful behaviour towards students.
- Treat all students with fairness and consistency.
- Be aware of how behaviour and language might be interpreted by students.
- Be aware of the possible implications of physical contact with students.
- Use language that is free of gender or cultural bias.
- Use positive imagery and language.

Islington Arts Factory

James Brindley Hospital School

Catford Girls School, Catford

People working together

Partnering

- Ensure that there is sufficient space for the activity, especially if it involves travelling.
- Encourage a sense of mutual care and responsibility between partners.
- Encourage spatial awareness, and orientation within the space and in relation to other dancers.

Weight-sharing

In addition to the points above:

- Facilitate a progressive development of understanding and skill. Start slowly and carefully with activities that allow students to maintain control of their own weight.
- Ensure students know how to complete the weight-sharing and recovery safely, and know what to do in case of difficulty.
- Develop mutual trust and confidence.
- Be aware that speed can increase the danger of accidents or injury.

- Encourage students to say if they are unsure or unhappy, and allow them to opt out of the activity if appropriate.
- Encourage students to reflect on their learning and articulate how they feel about the experience.

Supporting and lifting

In addition to the points above:

- Ensure students have sufficient strength and maturity to cope with the activity.
- Ensure students can demonstrate appropriate placement and alignment.
- Provide individual attention to ensure techniques are understood.
- Ensure students understand the need to maintain attention and concentration.
- Ensure students are alert to general and any relevant specific safety issues.

In Practice

Progression and Development

Examples of the ways that dance activities can grow.

Cando2 Integrated Youth Dance Company

I see Catherine, a wheelchair user, on the floor with Sara. They are singing into their mobile phones, arm bopping with the spare hand and crossing their legs in time to the music. Clare is contorting herself round Kimberley's wheelchair. Is Kimberley crying? No, she's laughing so much she can hardly wheel straight. And Nicki, who has an electric wheelchair, is helping Anna fall to the floor so she can finish the move in a body ripple, and then they both turn.

Cando2 is for young people of mixed abilities, aged 11 to 16. They are the group and therefore govern what they do. They take turns to be official group photographer, hair and make-up artists, keeper of the Radar Key and spokesperson for the group. These roles have given them an overwhelming sense of ownership. They came up with the name, T-shirt designs and help in the artistic direction and layout of the Cando2 website.

Over the last two years, I have watched these young adults grow in confidence. Their consideration for each other is impressive, and the way they juggle school, homework, other leisure activities and hanging around with their mates demonstrates amazing time management and prioritising skills. They explore movement, create, make up routines to their favourite songs and turn the music up full blast. It is a safe environment, free from sniggers if things go wrong, bullying or intimidating behaviour. As they grow up, I hope that this is how some of them remember the time they have spent in Cando2.

Some have already moved on and are still dancing. Laura, one of Cando2's early wheelchair users, is now working with Stop Gap Dance Company. Natasha has set up youth dance classes in her home town of Brighton, and Kimberley is aiming for a job with CandoCo organising youth projects. Wherever they go, the skills, confidence and experiences they have gained will be valuable and transferable. Young people grow up so quickly - some have to - but the few hours they spend with Cando2 enable them to be creative, expressive and 12 years old.

Pippa Stock, *CandoCo Youth Project Co-ordinator*

Rubicon Boys Dance Programme

Until 1988 there were very few boys dancing at Rubicon. Then an after-school boys session was started at Adamsdown Primary School with 25 boys aged between 8 and 11. A few months later, the sessions transferred to the Rubicon Centre, although the boys were rather anxious that their 'street cred' would go out the window if they were seen entering a dance centre.

After about a year of making their own dances and taking part in local events, boys from other schools were invited to join and the group became the Rubicon Boys Dance Group. They took part in performances, including at St David's Hall in Cardiff with the BBC National Orchestra of Wales. More recently the boys have made an energetic dance featuring their scooters. They performed it at Rubicon's 25th birthday performance and it proved such a hit that they went on to tour to five schools in Cardiff, performing and giving workshops.

Now there are two groups at Rubicon, one for 7 to 11 year-olds and one for 12 to 16 year-olds, and we are bursting at the seams. There are three other boys groups across the city of Cardiff: a total of 80 boys a week are dancing and we have plans to set up more boys groups. The original boys have been a fantastic inspiration to other boys wanting to have a go at dance.

Tracey Brown, *Dance Development Leader, Rubicon Dance Centre*

Bisakha Sarker: World Music Box

The World Music Box is an initiative by Liverpool Education Authority's Early Years Development and Childcare partnership for 60 pre-school nurseries and playgroups in the city. The aim of the project is to introduce the children, through music and dance, to the wider world that exists beyond their immediate environments.

A team of two artists visits each set-up to work with both the children and the staff. Music composer/practitioner Chris Davies leads the music section and I provide the dance input. The activities evolve round a box of about 30 musical instruments specially chosen for children aged two to four years. Each organisation gets a music box for a year and a workshop session with the artists.

My training and understanding of Indian dance, and experience of teaching dance in many unconventional settings, helped me to devise programmes of activities suitable for young children. I focus on enhancing the musicality of the children. They learn to move in response to the music, to listen for the musical cues and to develop a feel for different qualities of musical sounds.

A typical class starts with the children sitting in a circle on the floor. Most of the children follow us and take their shoes and socks off, although some feel secure with their socks on and a few will flatly refuse to remove their shoes. We clap hands, clap on different parts of the body, and on the carpet. We find patterns of different claps to introduce our names as an initial trust-building and warm-up exercise. I like to start by introducing the idea of 'Namaskar', the greetings ritual of Indian dance. I also use simple stories of friendship between the hands, the feet and the knees, to make them relax, laugh and be ready to get to the next stage of travelling, jumping and turning.

The most enjoyable parts are the short-story dances involving animals or trips to the park, set to the music played on the instruments from the box. We allocate different instruments to different animals, providing sound cues that the children learn to recognise. Many of the schools are intrigued by our practice of combining music and dance making, as they usually focus on one or the other. This project has once again made me realise the importance of finding a suitable language of instruction and appropriate imagery.

We leave assessment forms for the teachers to complete, but the true evaluation comes in the form of big smiles and big hugs with tiny little arms.

Bisakha Sarker

Ludus Dance Company: Boro-Ramizi Youth Centre, Pristina, Kosova

One of the keys to a successful dance workshop is to plan clear aims, objectives and desired outcomes. Prior knowledge of a group helps ensure appropriate aims and objectives are matched to the participants' needs. However, a recent workshop with breakdancers at the Boro-Ramizi Youth Group in Prishtina, Kosovo, certainly challenged the 'safety-net' of our familiar workshop methods and procedures.

During a week-long residency in Prishtina, organised and funded by the British Council, we performed our show CLASH, based on conflict-resolution, at the Kosovo National Theatre and delivered show-related workshops to performing arts students from the university. Some unexpected gaps appeared in the timetable, so we suggested offering a workshop at the local youth centre next to the British Council Offices. We had little information about the 30 young people who enthusiastically signed up for this workshop other than there was a core group keen on breakdancing and others who were interested in 'modern' and 'creative' dance.

We arrived early at the venue to check out the space, and found only three young men. Music was booming, the lino was out and we were amazed by a display of breakdancing – spins, windmills, flips and balances. They were skilled and the atmosphere was already exciting and welcoming. We discussed which sections of our repertory we could work with. Lots of partner work, with lifts, incorporating throwing and catching seemed appropriate, together with some martial arts style sequences from the conflict section of the show. The more physical and challenging the better, to develop their existing skills and to introduce new movement material that the dancers could perhaps integrate into their own repertoire.

The group was immediately 'hooked' by the warm-up, which was a lively travelling sequence along the floor. The sequence developed to involve energetic dives, rolls, jumps and catches. No-one wanted to stop! The skill, speed and enthusiasm of the group was incredible and we knew that we could really push things further and have a great time. Soon the group was performing martial arts-style duets based on use of weight, balance and intricate contact work, with strong focus, determination and precision.

In this atmosphere, our usual role as initiators was challenged. The energy and enthusiasm from the group became the driving force of the session, we were feeding off the group, trying to stay one step ahead of them, and introduce the next set of skills to be hungrily absorbed, practised and performed.

After the workshop and on reflection, we discussed the issue of planning. However much information we receive prior to a workshop, the unknown is always going to be the group itself. Whatever the situation, as facilitators we need to organise warm-up activities that allow us to assess each individual quickly in terms of confidence, motivation, skill, experience and ability to work as a group. We can organise a session and write detailed lesson plans outlining each single activity, but it is also important to be confident as teachers, to be flexible and respond spontaneously to the individuals and the group itself, allowing creativity to develop.

Kate Mercer, *Dancer/Teacher*
Gil Graystone, *Head of Touring*

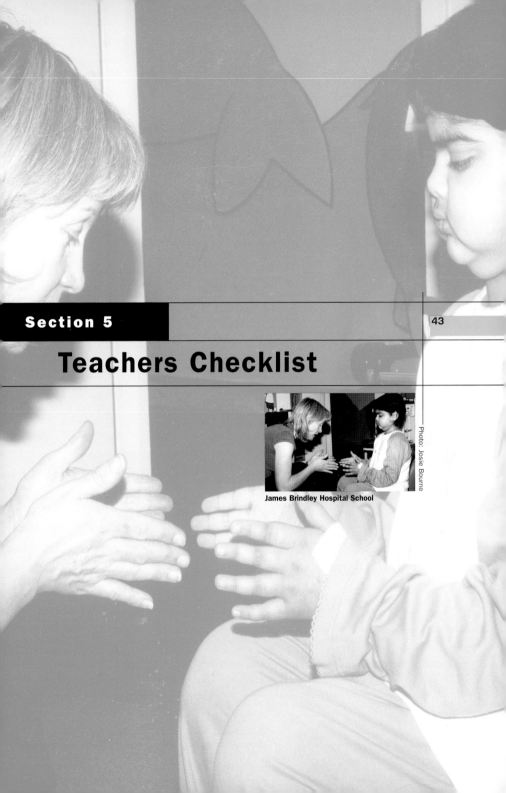

Teachers Checklist

James Brindley Hospital School

Photo: Josie Bourne

Some of the following points will be more important and relevant depending on the individual teacher's purpose and the specific teaching context. The checklist is divided into:

Before: planning and preparation for a class or workshop, or series of classes
During: strategies to promote learning during the class or workshop
After: reflecting and evaluating the success of the class or workshop in order to continually improve teaching practice and inform future planning and preparation

"Laura inspired me to work hard and I might try and do the same in Ms Coke's class."

Participant in Shobana Jeyasingh Dance Company's Half Term project

Photo: Vipul Sangoi

Anusha Subramanyam's Bharata Natyam class at the Patidar Samaj

Before

- Be clear about personal purpose, vision and values.
- If preparing for an examination, share the assessment criteria with students. It is helpful for students to understand what examiners are looking for.
- Be clear about teaching/learning objectives and plan to share these with students, ensuring that they understand.
- Think carefully (in consultation with parents and carers where appropriate) about the specific needs of children, for example those who may have emotional and behavioural difficulties, speech and language difficulties, attention deficit disorder or English as an additional language.
- Plan appropriate evaluation processes.
- Where relevant, review previous evaluations and/or the progress made during the last class.
- Plan teaching material to meet the objectives in the light of progress made previously, to promote the development of students, and to be progressive in content and level of challenge.
- Consider using a range of resources, stimuli, sources of inspiration, explanation and information, for example: pictures, videos, posters, music, anatomical diagrams, skeletons.

- Plan teaching material and strategies that are appropriate to the age and maturity of participants, their gender, cultural background, physique and different abilities, and to the genre, style or technique.
- Structure the class, thinking about the beginning, middle and end.
- Consider a variety of teaching strategies and the overall pace of the class.
- Allow time to introduce the material, to discuss teaching points, to provide and invite feedback from students, and for students to reflect and articulate their learning.
- Discuss aims, structure and content of the class, and each other's roles, with any colleagues, for example: assistants, musicians, dance artists, other teachers.
- Prepare music, videos and other resources, and any equipment required.
- Where necessary, ensure any travel or other arrangements are in place.
- Plan to arrive in good time for the start of the class, to check the space is open and ready for the session - clear, clean, warm, well-ventilated and light - or to allow time to adapt the class if necessary.
- Warm up before students arrive.

Cando2

Photo: John Cole

During

Getting started

- Welcome students.
- Keep a register of names, addresses and contact phone numbers, and keep it up to date.
- If working with a group for the first time, introduce yourself, consider students introducing themselves and using name labels so that you can use their names wherever possible.
- Ask whether everyone is in good health and injury free; be prepared to adjust material and strategies if necessary.
- Share and agree your aims with the participants.
- Ensure everyone is warmed up. It can be useful to include movements in the warm up that will be developed later in the session.
- Encourage participants to bring water into class and prompt regular re-hydration.

Strategies

- Always check for understanding - do not assume instructions and explanations are clear.
- Use students' names and maintain eye contact as much as possible, especially when giving feedback; make sure that everyone in the class receives positive comments and attention at some time.
- Use a variety of teaching strategies, including instructions and explanations that require auditory, visual, emotional and kinaesthetic responses.
- Use a variety of imagery to inspire and explain; encourage participants to imagine succeeding in all tasks.
- Provide background information, for example descriptions of how the body works anatomically, the purpose of the specific exercise or task.
- Make reference to choreographers and dance works.
- If working with musicians, involve them in the class and its aims and objectives.
- Face the class and 'mirror' students.
- Use demonstration to clarify tasks and teaching points; combine teacher demonstration with asking participants to demonstrate.

East London Dance/Random Dance Company

Photo: Pau Ros

Photo: Jason Budge

Vincent Dance Theatre

- Provide a context for specific tasks and help participants understand its purpose or where it is leading.
- Teach 'whole, part, whole': begin with the whole sequence, then focus on particular movements or sections, then the whole sequence again.
- Maintain a balanced pace of class so that there is a mixture of 'small detail' and 'big picture' work.
- Teach the whole group and individuals within the group.
- Change the combinations in which participants work, for example, individually, in pairs, and in different sizes of group.
- Discourage participants from having a preferred place at the barre or in the studio; rotate the lines of the class regularly.
- Be aware of your own 'geography' in class – use the whole teaching area.
- Involve any students who may be watching, due to injury, to participate and feel a valued part of the class.
- Occasionally cover up mirrors.
- Use plenty of positive comments and images throughout the class.
- Give lots of praise and constructive feedback - be specific about what is done well and why it is good.
- Encourage input from participants, and encourage them to articulate their views, responses and learning.
- Avoid language that is gender or culture specific or could be considered abusive.
- Encourage, encourage, encourage!

After

- Review the aim or goal of the class.
- Find an appropriate time to discuss the results of examinations and any feedback provided by the examiner.
- Encourage participants to reflect on what was accomplished, comment on successful teaching strategies and remind them of their progress.
- Be available after the class in case anyone wants specific advice or to ask a question or make a comment.
- Note any particular successes or problems for future consideration.
- Keep up to date and inspired; take advantage of professional development opportunities.

Evaluation

Some classes, workshops and projects will require detailed or specific evaluation. In these cases, planning for evaluation needs to be built into planning for the sessions. For example, will participants feedback verbally or fill in evaluation forms? At what point(s) will they provide feedback? Suggested publications about evaluation are included in *Resources*.

The results of evaluation informs future planning, approaches and strategies. A sample checklist for teachers' continuing self-evaluation is included in *Resources*.

In Practice

Dance and Technology

Examples of collaborations.

Dance 4, Nottingham
Time: **dance and film project with young people at risk**

Exploring the themes of crime and crime prevention, and shot within and around the historic buildings of the Galleries of Justice in Nottingham, *Time* is a short film made in the space of a week by 12 young people who were at risk of offending. With funding from First Light, a lottery funded Film Council initiative, Dance 4 teamed up with new partners including an independent film-maker, a film production agency, a Youth Offending Team, the Galleries of Justice and the Youth Service.

The project aimed to engage the group in a creative project to explore issues of concern to them and work in an inspiring environment. For Dance 4, it provided a new way of engaging with young people. Choreography was used as the 'story-telling' process, and movement was then explored in small groups using photography and video to encourage a greater visual awareness and appreciation of overall style. Each participant had access to equipment, was shown how to use it and how to experiment with angle, focus and mood. The camera was an alternative choreographic tool, pushing participants to experience new ways of communicating with each other and generating dance for a non-live context. The wide range of professionals encouraged independent thinking and decision making by the participants.

The final result was an eight-minute film that brought together a collection of images created by the young people. It responded to the location and expressed their preoccupations and concerns for their future lives.

Louise Bardgett, *Education and Community Manager*

Scottish Youth Dance (YDance)

YDance is developing a multimedia resource for primary and secondary schools. The ABCD (Any Body Can Dance) CD-Rom uses new technology to provide information and advice for teachers and young people. The project began when Scottish Youth Dance received National Lottery funding from the Scottish Arts Council to develop new teachers' packs. Rather than create a conventional pack, it was decided to develop a resource that could be used more creatively and flexibly by teachers in a range of contexts. The initial concept was developed by a creative team of Andy Howitt, Artistic Director of Scottish Youth Dance, Maggie Singleton, Glasgow City Council's Officer for Children and Young People and John Anderson, Director of CodeBlue Multimedia.

The ABCD Rom allows teachers the opportunity to explore dance with a range of applications including:
• Information on Scottish Youth Dance
• Advice Bank
• Email and other related links
• Hints, questions and practical points in teaching dance
• Dance Planner
• Movement games, workshop ideas and warm-up exercises using 3-D animation and teacher handouts
• Video footage and photos of children dancing
• Dance combination builder
• Music maker

The ABCD Rom provides suggested class plans, choreography step-by-step, games and the tools necessary to build a class or a whole programme of dance. It also enables teachers to make and save dance combinations, music, class plans and choreography. Information built using the ABCD Rom can be saved and recalled by any user so that, over time, a library of work can be built up which can then be emailed and traded with other ABCD Rom users.

The ABCD Rom is currently undergoing testing, and initial feedback from teachers and artists involved in the test-phase has been extremely positive, "I have seen the future, and it works", Robert Livingston, Director Hi – Arts. YDance plan to release the final version of the ABCD Rom in August 2002.

Andy Howitt, *Artistic Director Scottish Youth Dance*

Vincent Dance Theatre
Orbital

Orbital was a week-long residency by Vincent Dance Theatre, which took place in Bridlington, Yorkshire, in April 2002. The residency combined work in dance, music, digital technology and skateboarding with 12 young males aged 12-18. The participants had no previous dance experience, but were very committed and interested in skateboarding. Some had been excluded from school and suffered from behavioural problems. The project's Artistic Director was Charlotte Vincent. She was supported by film makers Jason Budge and Michael Akerman, DJ Lloyd and Kirsty Readhead, the Dance Development Officer of East Riding.

During the residency, the participants explored ways of combining dance with skateboarding. The week included film and DJ workshops, and opportunities for the young men to record and make their own work on film. The participants particularly liked this aspect of the project and enjoyed filming their own version of *Baywatch*. They also appreciated the opportunity to work with a professional DJ. The residency resulted in a site-specific performance at Bridlington Funfair, a video, a CD of the soundtrack and a live TV broadcast.

Orbital was important as it began to break down exclusion barriers. Involving young socially excluded males in a dance project was ambitious; dance is not something that would normally appeal to this group. By tailoring the residency around the group's interest in skateboarding, their interest was maintained. Allowing the participants to take charge of the camera gave them a sense of responsibility and ownership; being trusted with equipment raised the group's self-esteem. The participants enjoyed taking part in the performance as it provided them with an opportunity to display the skills that they had learnt. It also allowed the people of Bridlington to see that these young males could make a positive contribution to the area, instead of vandalising it.

Orbital was a successful project for Vincent Dance Theatre and it made a positive contribution towards raising low levels of self-esteem in the group by equipping its members with transferable skills. But the biggest breakthrough the project made was enabling these young males to make a positive contribution to Bridlington.

Charlotte Vincent, Artistic Director

The Legal Framework

Cando2

Photo: John Cole

*"I enjoy jumping and turning and I
like dancing because it is energetic. I
enjoy doing something new and I might
get a chance to perform or do
something I haven't done before."*

Nicholas Brown, participant in
Birmingham Royal Ballet's Dance
Track programme

Photo: Merlin Hendy

**RAD postgraduate degree student teaching at
Crawley Infant School**

There is a broad range of legislation that affects dance teachers. For a teacher or parent, knowing what is relevant and what action should be taken is a daunting task. As far as the law is concerned, dance teachers might be providing childcare, be responsible for premises, be businesses, employers and licensees. Different pieces of legislation will affect teachers depending upon how, when, where and whom they teach. The purpose of this section is to outline a broad legal framework affecting those teaching dance in different settings. It will focus on two main areas: working with children and business/professional requirements.

Working with children

The past twelve years has seen an increase in the amount of legislation designed to protect children from harm. The Children Act 1989 broadly defines harm as "ill treatment or the impairment of health or development." This definition includes physical, intellectual, emotional, social and behavioural development; physical and mental health and any form of abuse (not just sexual abuse).

More recently the law has been focused on those who work with children, ensuring that those 'unsuitable' for this type of work may be identified and aiming to protect children from being placed in potentially abusive and dangerous situations. Legislation affecting dance teachers includes, amongst others, *The UN Convention on the Rights of the Child, Children Act 1989, Human Rights Act 1998, Protection of Children Act 1999, The Care Standards Act 2000, Criminal Justice and Courts Act 2000* and the *Disability Discrimination Act 2001.*

Much of this legislation is designed for organisations or individuals whose main aim is to care for children (for example nurseries or childminders). It is important that those teaching dance, and working with children, are aware of the culture and know some of the regulations that might affect their professional practice. Teachers need to understand their legal duties to those they teach.

Duty of care
The first point to note is that teachers are in a position of trust and owe a 'duty of care' to their students. It is reasonable for a dance student to expect that their teacher is competent to teach dance. While this might seem obvious, it will be the first question asked if something goes wrong. If a child is injured and parents claim that a teacher acted negligently, that teacher will be judged against the standard of a 'reasonable professional'.

Photo: Roy Peters for Peppy Hills

SUNMOVES a land based arts project

Child protection

The Acts referred to cover the protection of children in general under English law (Scotland has comparable but slightly different legislation). Understanding the legislation and its impact on a dance teacher can be difficult. There are two main areas that affect those working with children.

First is the issue of caring for children. In relation to Part Xa of the Children Act 1989, organisations and individuals providing the care of children must be registered. The registration authority for England is OFSTED (HM Chief Inspector of Schools). For those teaching dance (or music or sports) the care provided is considered usually to be incidental. In other words, that teachers are looking after children during their dance class or workshop is inevitable, but not the main purpose of holding classes. This is not a hard and fast rule and whether or not a teacher or school should be registered with OFSTED will depend upon the age of the children, the length of time the child spends there and the frequency of the provision. Generally speaking, dance teachers do not need to be registered.

Second, teachers must be fit to work with children. This issue is covered by several pieces of legislation, notably the Protection of Children Act 1999 (PoCA) and the Criminal Justice and Courts Act 2000 (CJCA). Under CJCA it is a criminal offence for someone to apply for or accept any work if he or she is disqualified from working with children. It is also a criminal offence to employ someone disqualified or not to remove someone from post who is disqualified (for example someone with a criminal record for the abuse of children). CJCA also attempts to define what is meant by 'working with children' and dance teachers, along with sports and voluntary groups are likely to be included in that definition. The Protection of Children Act also aims to identify those unsuitable to work with children but focuses more closely on child care organisations. Dance teachers and those employing them are not required to undertake checks but it is considered to be good practice. Essentially, such checks establish that a named person is not included on any of the disqualification lists.

The Criminal Records Bureau has developed a scheme to consolidate the different lists and conduct checks. The scheme is called Disclosure. Organisations must first register to use the scheme and then there is a charge of approximately £12 per record checked. This charge is waived for volunteers. In Scotland, the Scottish Criminal Records Office checks records.

- Teachers should be aware that they might be subject to such a check.
- If a school, company or agency is employing people to work with children, it needs to be aware of the developments in legislation in this area and be prepared to conduct checks if that is the requirement.

Photo: Jason Budge

Vincent Dance Theatre

Further information
Further information is available. Many sports bodies have provided guidance child protection policies, which state what a teacher will do should he or she suspect a child is suffering from abuse. It is good practice for a teacher to establish such a policy. Useful information and guidance may be obtained from:

NSPCC
The NSPCC has a wide range of advice and information about working with children and child protection. There is a specialist Child Protection in Sport Unit, which produces relevant publications.
helpline: 0808 800 5000
web: www.nspcc.org.uk

Criminal Records Bureau and Disclosure
The CRB website and helpline provides information about the various listings and how to go about getting checks.
info line: 0870 9090811
web: www.disclosure.gov.uk

Publications
Creating Safety: Child Protection Guidelines for the Arts, produced by Scottish Arts Council in partnership with Children in Scotland. Available online: www.sac.org.uk or call the help desk: 0845 603 6000

Protection of Children Act: A Practical Guide to the Act for all Organisations working with Children, available from Department of Health, PO Box 777, London, SE1 6XH or online: www.doh.gov.uk/scg/childprotect

Protecting Children: a guide for sportspeople, published by NSPCC and sports coach UK

Child Protection Procedures and Practices Handbook, published by the Football Association

Copies of the legislation are available free online from www.legislation.hmso.gov.uk/acts

Business and professional requirements

Dance organisations, schools and teachers are also small businesses. As such, there is a range of employment and professional legal requirements that they must meet. The list that follows is not exhaustive, but focuses on areas where advice and information is most often sought.

Contracts
It is important for dance schools, agencies and other employers to make sure that on-going arrangements with teachers are on a formal footing. This protects both parties if something goes wrong. A contract should include the following:

• Agreed activity or job description
• Agreed hours of work
• Working time agreement or exclusion
• Agreed place of employment
• Agreed rate of pay
• Agreed period of employment
• Agreed holiday entitlement
• Provision in case of sickness (if any)
• Notice period

It is worth remembering that a contract does not have to be written for it to be binding. It clarifies matters for both parties if there is a written record of the terms of employment. Employers are legally obliged to ensure that the work environment and practices are safe and will not cause physical or psychological damage to their employees. An employer may not exclude his liability in this area (ie a contract cannot state that the employer will not be responsible for any accident or harm caused by faulty equipment etc).

Photo: Tom Martin

Dance 4

Photo: slater-king.com

St Magdalens R.C. Primary School, Brockley

There is a wide range of employment legislation. It is worth obtaining a guide to key issues such as those produced by ACAS and Business Link.

Employment Guides for Small Firms – fact sheet pack produced by ACAS and the Small Business Service available by email: publications@dti.gsi.gov.uk or call 0870 150 2500.

Data Protection

In accordance with the Data Protection Act 1998 everyone has a right to see information held about him or her by another organisation. Depending upon the type of data kept an organisation may have to register (eligibility can be checked online www.dataprotection.gov.uk). A fee may be charged to anyone wishing to see records. A teacher does not have the right to use information provided by students or staff as he or she wishes, for example, it is illegal to pass it on to a third party without the student or parent's permission. However, the teacher may need to pass on some information (for example information required by examination bodies). A teacher or organisation

should have a policy about data protection and inform parents and students of this.

Disability Discrimination Act 1995

There is a range of legislation that supports equal opportunities. One of the most recent pieces of legislation is the Disability Discrimination Act (DDA). The DDA introduces new measures aimed at ending discrimination faced by many disabled people. Attention is drawn to this act because studios and dance organisations may have to implement changes to meet the requirements of this legislation. Furthermore, the DDA has been modified by the Special Educational Needs and Disability Act 2001.

Dance teaching is likely to be covered by two areas in the DDA. First, under Part 3, dance teachers may be classed as service providers. Service providers must ensure that disabled people do not receive less favourable treatment and they must make reasonable adjustments to ensure that their services are accessible to disabled people. From October 2004, this will include ensuring that buildings are accessible.

Birmingham Royal Ballet Soloist, Lee Fisher, working with Fox Hollies School, Birmingham

Photo: Adrian Burrows

From September 2002 educational bodies, including state and independent schools, further and higher education institutions will have a duty to make reasonable adjustments ensuring accessibility. From 2003, post-16 educational establishments will also have to provide auxiliary aids and services to disabled people.

The Disability Rights Commission has a website and a helpline staffed by specialists: www.drc-gb.org, telephone 08457 622 633. DRC staff know the relevant legislation and have education experts who can advise on the impact of the DDA and what adjustments should be made. The DRC also produces email newsletters providing regular updates.

Insurance

As dance teachers are working with the public, it is important that they hold the appropriate insurance policies. Teachers will have to decide which policies best suit their needs.

First is public liability insurance. All teachers should hold this insurance or ensure that the building in which they teach is covered. This protects teachers from claims from members of the public for death, illness, injury, loss or damage to property. Some, but not all, policies will exclude liability for professional negligence, for example if a student is injured during class and the teacher is deemed to have been negligent. The majority of policies provide cover for up to £2 million.

Professional indemnity insurance can provide cover against liability for negligence. This can include not only an individual teacher but also his or her employees.

Personal Accident insurance may be useful to a teacher to protect him or herself against injury.

There is a range of brokers offering different insurance packages. Several organisations offer specialist insurance to their members, for example, Dance UK, Equity and several teaching organisations offer such policies. These group schemes may offer insurance at a cheaper price because of the numbers of people covered.

Photo: Anthony Brannan

Scottish Youth Dance

Music and performing rights licences

The use of live and recorded music in dance classes and performances is covered by copyright law. Teachers need to obtain appropriate licences or ensure that the premises in which they are teaching or performing hold such licences. The fees paid for music copyright licences provide royalties to record companies, composers and songwriters.

There are two types of licence a teacher should hold, or ensure is held by the venue:

Performing right licence. If music is played outside a domestic sphere, the business or individual must have a licence (for example, if a radio is turned on in an office, a licence is required). Whether or not a teacher needs a licence to cover, for example, a performance in a community hall or theatre depends upon whether the venue holds a licence. Teachers should always check. Performing right licences are issued by the **Performing Rights Society (PRS),** which collects and distributes the royalties. Some dance teaching organisations that produce printed or taped music (for example the Royal Academy of Dance) have waived their collection rights with PRS. When a teacher or school makes a declaration, they can exclude use of this music from their licence.

Phonographic Performance Ltd (PPL) licence. PPL issues licences and collects royalties in relation to particular recordings of music. Generally to play current CDs or other recordings a teacher will need to hold a PPL licence. There are exemptions to this rule. For example, educational charities may not have to pay for a licence if the proceeds of an event go back into the charity. However, this should be checked with PPL.

Both PRS and PPL have very useful websites and information helplines. They are familiar with the requirements of dance organisations. If in doubt about whether a licence is necessary or appropriate, check with both organisations.

Phonographic Performance Ltd
1 Upper James Street
London
W1R 3HG
tel: 020 8664 4400
web: www.ppluk.com

Performing Rights Society
29-33 Berners Street
London
W1T 3AB
switchboard: 020 7580 5544
helpline (for guidance): 08000 684828
web: www.prs.co.uk

Notes on other professional matters
Dance teaching is not yet a regulated profession. Dance teachers are affected by a number of rules and regulations but these tend to be incidental to their role as teachers. Only those working in statutory education will be subject to specific legislation.

The lack of regulation does not mean that teachers should not pay attention to professional requirements. This book sets out guidance on good practice for teachers in a variety of settings. Teachers should endeavour to ensure that they have the professional competence to teach dance. In addition to the publications listed throughout this section CDET's *Code of professional conduct and standards of good practice for dance teachers* and Dance UK's *A Dancer's Charter* provide some guidance.

In Practice

Learning and Language

Examples of dance promoting language.

The Place Learning and Access: Dancing the Words

Dancing the Words aims to develop children's language and conceptual understanding through dance lessons linked to their science curriculum. The project is led by Education Officer Lucy Moelwyn-Hughes and a team of dance specialists. It is run in partnership with Winton Primary School in King's Cross, London where for many pupils English is an additional language which they may rarely speak at home.

Head Teacher Jane Fulford highlights the benefits of this approach:

"Dancing the properties of liquids and solids, or creating a 'rainbow rap' about the qualities of light, has given children a deeper and longer-lasting understanding of difficult concepts. It has helped them to develop socially and physically, while also having fun."

The project involves five Year 3, 4, and 5 classes. This places great demands on the class teachers, but the partnership has been highly successful :

"It's been really good for us as teachers. It's helped us to see different ways of delivering lessons, different approaches to teaching. It's been nice for the kids to see us working alongside teachers that aren't part of the school and to see us working so closely."
Leigh Derbyshire, Class Teacher

"The fact that the knowledge is being reinforced through the movement reaches children that may not have been included in the learning process." Reuben Moses, Class Teacher

"For me the most positive aspect is realising that science learning, music and movement can all be used to enhance one another. For the children, they're actually beginning to realise now that what they're doing is learning, and that learning is fun, and it goes back into the classroom." Wendy Chaffe, Year 3/4 Science Co-ordinator

The pupils also appreciate a different way of learning:

"We use dance to help us understand our science lessons in a different way."

"Learning about something using your body, as well as your brain, is a really helpful way to remember things."

Dancing the Words is funded by the Department for Education and Skills, The Cripplegate Foundation and the Reta Lila Howard Foundation, which is assisting with the costs of evaluation and dissemination.

Christopher Thomson, *Learning and Access, The Place*

Judith Palmer: Movement and Music in Conversation

Judith's aim in this workshop was for the Year 4 and 5 children, including some with a visual impairment, to gain a personal understanding of drum language.

Time was spent on developing listening skills, hearing the drum beat which 'talks' and signals the movement sequence, using the conventions of the relationship between drummer and dancer in African dance to coax the dancer from within each child by immersing them in the drum language.

The children learnt one particular movement involved in African dance, through exercises in dipping and arching of the back and thrusting forward of the chest. Mimicry of animal movements is an aspect of African dance that children readily relate to, and each movement was voiced rhythmically before being physically demonstrated to include the visually impaired children. In this way the children learnt the movement of the Tokwe dance and developed a sequence. Farhana, one of the visually impaired students, developed a real understanding of the dance and was the 'anchor' for the line formation.

The class and the support teacher took part in the sessions and the dance became the class project. The Tokwe dance from Ghana was performed for the school assembly and for parents.

Judith Palmer

Powys Dance: Telling Tales/Dweud Chwedlau

Telling Tales aimed to facilitate integration between pupils and staff from Brecon Schools and Coleg Powys through a dance performance project. The lead school, Ysgol Penmaes, caters for pupils with moderate and severe disabilities. They elected to link with age appropriate groups from Mount St Junior School Learning Support Class, Brecon High School and Access students from Coleg Powys with and without disabilities.

Three pieces were created, each taking a local myth as a stimulus. The pieces were linked through tri-lingual narration: Welsh, English and Makaton. Although the majority of the participants were English speaking, one group worked exclusively through the mediums of Welsh and Makaton, with the result that everyone involved developed a selective vocabulary in the new languages and the confidence to use these skills to communicate with each other.

Each group worked for approximately 16 hours over an eight-week period. Fabulous props and costumes, which were made and used during the rehearsal process with the guidance of Arts Alive, added an essential element to the visual impact of the finished work. Teachers and support staff worked as members of the group contributing creatively to the process. The project culminated in a performance at Theatr Brycheiniog, a modern professional venue with full technical support. Over 100 performers shared their achievements with an audience of friends and family.

Heidi Wilson

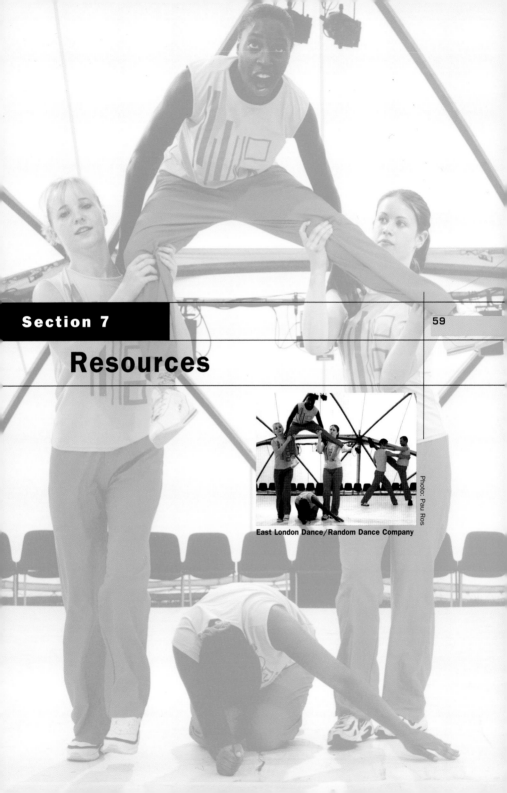

Resources

East London Dance/Random Dance Company

Photo: Pau Ros

Safe Dance Practice for Children and Young People

Jill Elbourn

Dance teachers should ensure their practice is safe, effective and appropriate and should be able to assess risks associated with exercises or movements included in their classes or in choreographed pieces.

Assessing risk focuses on whether an exercise is appropriate for the person performing it and whether it complies with principles of safe practice in relation to impact, joint alignment and control.

When working with young dancers, teachers should know and understand the physiological issues which affect the response of children and young people to exercise as well as the issues associated with the three principles of safe exercise practice.

The tables on pages 61-63 summarise key facts concerning children (aged 5-10 years) and young people's (aged 11-18 years) physical development. These age groups have been selected for simplification. Each table describes the movement implications, including the possible risks associated with each key fact and provides suggestions for safe practice.

The tables on pages 64-66 describe the principles of safe exercise practice associated with impact, alignment and control. Each table describes risk implications associated with poor practice and includes recommendations for minimising these risks.

The table on page 67 describes some of the risks to health and safety for young people who are involved in very intense training.

Photo: Kevin Low

Scottish Dance Theatre, *High Land*

Children (aged 5–10 years)

Key Facts	Implications	Safe Practice
The growth plate at the ends of children's bones is weak and soft.	Children's bones are more susceptible to injury, especially the ends of the bones where the growth plate is situated.	Avoid activities which put the bones and joints under excessive strain, e.g. deep knee bends on landing from jumps, excessive jumping (especially on concrete floors without protective footwear).
Children's body proportions differ from adults (e.g. bottom heavy with a weak upper body and big head). They also have a weaker mid-section.	A child's weak mid-section can struggle to support their weight especially during actions that involve long levers, e.g. the upper body.	Avoid exercises which incorporate long levers, e.g. bending to the side from a standing position with both arms overhead.
Children have a lower rate of sweat production and a higher rate of heat production than adults. They also have a larger ratio of body surface area to weight.	Children cannot regulate their body temperature as efficiently as adults (i.e. they heat up rapidly during exercise, overheat easily and lose heat rapidly in cold conditions).	In hot conditions encourage children to wear light clothing, reduce exercise intensity and provide frequent rest periods. Plenty of fluids should be available. In cold conditions encourage children to wear adequate layers of clothing and keep sessions as active as possible. Monitor children for signs of overheating or onset of hypothermia.
Children have less carbohydrate stored in their muscles than adults and a reduced ability to use it for energy.	Children are less efficient at performing short burst, high intensity (anaerobic) activities than adults.	High intensity activities (e.g. jumping) should be short and intermittent with adequate periods of recovery.

Young People (aged 11–18 years)

Key Facts	Implications	Safe Practice
Young people do not perceive steady paced activities (i.e. aerobic activities) to be strenuous.	Young people might continue to exercise when they are becoming fatigued.	Monitor young people to ensure that they do not work to the point of exhaustion when involved in sustained activity that lasts for long periods of time.
The potential of young people to perform intense, explosive activities (anaerobic activities), e.g. jumps, leaps or fast travelling, is less than that of adults.	Young people will tire quickly when involved in intense, explosive activities and are unable to perform these activities as efficiently as adults.	Ensure that young people are given sufficient time to recover before repeating or attempting to improve performance in intense, explosive activities.
At puberty young people experience alterations to their limb length and centre of gravity (e.g. girls develop longer backs, wider hips, narrower shoulders, and a lower centre of gravity than boys).	Young people might experience feelings of 'clumsiness', loss of confidence and self-esteem or may cause themselves harm by attempting to replicate skills that they were capable of performing prior to a growth spurt.	Encourage and help young people in a sensitive and progressive manner to relearn skills after a growth spurt (if appropriate) and help them to understand the temporary regression in their performance.
In adolescence bone growth occurs in the cartilage of epiphyseal plates in the long bones. These growth plates are vulnerable to injury, which can lead to permanent damage in growing bones.	On rare occasions the growth plate can be injured through: • repetitive compressive loads (e.g. taking body weight on hands in falling activities, excessive jumping and landing) • joints being used or placed repeatedly in incorrect alignment (e.g. knees hyperextending in first/second position, jumping in deep knee bend position) • performance of exercises in a rapid an uncontrolled manner (e.g. ballistic stretching).	Monitor technique to ensure that exercises are performed with control and using joints in correct alignment.

Young people of the same age and sex may be at very different stages of growth.	It might not be possible for all young people in a class to perform an exercise or movement at the same intensity, duration and/or level.	Enable young people to work at a level/intensity that is most appropriate for them as an individual.
Following a growth spurt young people's muscles will be relatively thin, weak and tight.	This may result in: • restricted range of movement around some joints • an imbalance between flexibility and strength which may result in poor joint alignment and muscles being more vulnerable to injury • an exaggerated pull on the tendon-bone insertion causing damage to a growth point (apophysis) where the tendon attaches to the muscle. This can lead to Osgood Schlatter's disease (below knee) or Sever's disease (in the heel). These conditions are common in young people who participate very frequently in one sport.	During the periods of active growth encourage and help young people to: • develop flexibility and muscular strength and endurance in the main muscle groups in order to reduce muscle tightness, avoid muscle imbalance, and maintain their range of movement about joints • perform exercises with correct alignment of joints • avoid excessive repetition of specific joint movements (e.g. kicking, jumping, running). Do not allow young people to participate if in pain.
The potential of boys to perform steady paced activity (aerobic activity) increases dramatically at puberty (approx. 12-14 years) and continues to increase rapidly until approximately the age of 16 after which increase is less rapid until approximately the age of 18.	While the aerobic potential of young men increases dramatically during puberty, their performance may be impaired by the conditions that commonly accompany periods of rapid bone growth (e.g. growing pains, periods of extreme tiredness, feelings of clumsiness and restricted range of movement about joints).	Be aware of the conditions that accompany rapid bone growth and their potential to impair aerobic potential, and respond sympathetically to young people who are genuinely experiencing these conditions.
The potential of girls to perform steady paced activity (aerobic activity) reaches its highest level between 10-12 years after which there is a rapid decline during puberty and a more steady decline through life. This decline in aerobic potential is related to an increase in the percentage of body fat.	Many young women will experience failure and loss of self-esteem if they are set aerobic tasks which are too challenging and which do not take into account the physiological reasons for their decline in performance.	Be aware of the complex reasons for the decline in aerobic performance of young women and adjust classes/dances to include activities which are challenging and motivating but which take account of this decline.
Girls reach their peak strength at the end of the growth spurt (age approx 13/14). Boys do not reach peak strength until one year after the end of the growth spurt (age approx 15/16).	There is a high risk of soft tissue injury (e.g. muscle pulls, tendinitis, cramps) as well as injury to the lower back, associated with young people performing dance moves (e.g. lifts) which demand maximal strength and power before peak strength has been reached.	Young people should not be involved in performing activities that demand maximal strength and power (e.g. lifts) until they have reached peak strength.

Principles of Safe Exercise Practice

Issue	Description	Risk Implications of High Impact Activities	Recommendations for Minimising Risk
Impact	Impact refers to force exerted against the floor. A high impact activity involves a great amount of force acting against the floor as in landing from a jump. High impact weight bearing activities stimulate healthy bone growth and development. Low impact activity involves a small amount of force acting against the floor, as in walking. Not all low impact activities involve one foot remaining in contact with the floor (e.g. stamping the feet increases impact).	Excessive high impact activity may result in shin splints, tendonitis, and tibial and fibial stress fractures. Excessive high impact might involve: • A series of jumping exercises placed consecutively in a class • Repetitive rehearsal of parts of a dance involving jumping Risk is increased when these activities are performed with poor technique and/or on hard floors.	Dance teachers/choreographers should: • provide sprung floors, or floors with a resilient surface • encourage safe take-off and landing technique • discourage young dancers from performing excessive amounts of high impact activity • alternate high impact and low impact activities • promote dances which comprise a good balance of high and low impact activities.

Principles of Safe Exercise Practice

Issue	Description	Risk Implications of Incorrect Alignment	Recommendations for Minimising Risk
ALIGNMENT	Placing and or moving joints in anatomically correct positions/ways. **CORRECT ALIGNMENT** Knees • 'Knees over toes' when performing pliés, landing from jumps • Seated hamstring stretch with resting leg bent and foot flat on the floor • Angle of knee joint not less than 90 degrees when landing from jumps, or performing lunges or hip flexor stretch • Not locking knees out when extending the legs, e.g. when standing in first/second position Spine • Tall spine, abdominal muscles pulled through to spine (e.g. posture) • Upper body twists to mobilise thoracic area of spine **INCORRECT ALIGNMENT** Knees • 'Knocking inwards' eg when performing plié • 'Hurdles' hamstring stretch • Hyperflexion (deep knee bends) eg when landing from jumps, performing lunges or hip flexor stretch • Hyperextension (locking out), e.g. when standing in 1st/2nd position Spine • Hyperflexion, e.g. legs over head from lying on back • Hyperextension, e.g. extreme back arching • Activities that attempt to rotate the lumbar region Elbows • Hyperextending elbows while they are supporting body weight	Poor joint alignment may place strain on ligament and tendon insertions. These are often situated near the weak epiphyseal growth plates at the ends of the bones. Repetitive strain during periods of growth may lead to joint laxity (instability). Hyperflexion and hyperextension of the spine may result (over a long period of time) in displacement of discs which can lead to back pain and restricted movement.	Dance teachers/choreographers should: • know and understand the range of motion about the joints and ensure that joints are moved and placed in anatomically correct positions/ways • use teaching points and demonstrations which help dancers to perform exercises with correct alignment • help young dancers to understand the safety issues associated with joint alignment and know how to check their own and others' exercise technique • substitute and/or refine technique of exercises which do not place or move joints in alignment.

Principles of Safe Exercise Practice

Issue	Description	Risk Implications of Performing Exercises Without Control	Recommendations for Minimising Risk
CONTROL	Performing exercises/activities in a 'smooth', careful manner. **Exercises performed with control** For example: • 'Placing' the arms during swinging, circling, mobility exercises in warm up • Controlled performance of side bends and upper body twists • Holding stretches still • Controlled 'lifting' and 'lowering' phases when performing strengthening exercises e.g. curl up, back raise **Exercises performed without control** For example using momentum when performing these: • Arm circles in a warm up (rotating arms furiously) • Curl ups (ricocheting off the mat) • Upper body twists (uncontrolled rotation) • Stretches (bouncing at the end of the muscle range) • Curl ups and back raises ('fling and drop')	Uncontrolled warm up exercises take muscles to the end of their range, at speed, while they are cold and at their least pliable. Injury to the muscle, tendon or tendon insertion may result. In young people tendon insertions are often situated close to the vulnerable growth plates. Following a growth spurt young people may: • have tight and relatively weak muscles which are particularly susceptible to injury caused by momentum • not be able to control the performance of exercises which involve long levers (e.g. curl ups/back raises with hands at side of head) Ballistic stretches and performing resistance exercises with momentum may cause minute or more acute muscle tears which can lead to stiffness, soreness and decreased pliability.	Dance teachers/choreographers should: • use teaching points and demonstrations which help young people to perform exercises with control • help young people to understand the safety issues associated with performing exercises with control and know how to check their own and others' technique • not expect all young people to achieve the same range of motion about joints and allow for those with tight and weak muscles by providing alternative exercises when appropriate.

Risks to Young People's Health and Safety Associated with Intense Training

Risks to Young People's Health and Safety Associated with Intense Training	Examples of Causes	Recommendations for Minimising Risk
Stress fractures - a bone crack caused by continual repetitive pressure from a muscle, muscle group or tendon pulling against a bone.	Abrupt increases in amount of training; training on inappropriate surfaces, e.g. concrete or unsprung floors; poor technique, e.g. in landing from jumps	Increase amount of training gradually, train on appropriate floors and surfaces, use appropriate footwear, use good technique, e.g. when landing from jumps.
Epiphyseal plate injuries - premature growth plate closure, which can result in bone deformity, joint disease and stunt the bone's growth.	Repetitive compressive loads, e.g. to lower back, knees caused by excessive jumping/lifting.	Ensure that young people vary training and activities.
Apophyseal injuries - damage to a growth point where a tendon attaches to the bone - caused by exaggerated pull on the tendon-bone insertion e.g. Sever's disease (insertion of the Achilles tendon into the calcaneous); Osgood-Schlatter's disease (insertion of patellar tendons into tibial tubercle just below the knee).	Overuse (e.g. repetitive and/or excessive jumping) combined with tightness of muscles immediately after a growth spurt.	Ensure that flexibility exercises are part of the training programme. Encourage young people to vary their training programme to avoid excessive repetition of specific joint movements, e.g. kicking, jumping, running. Do not allow young people to participate if in pain.
Disruption to menstrual cycle - which results from chronically low levels of oestrogen - the condition may prevent the attainment of peak bone mass and promote the development of stress fractures and scoliosis (curvature of the spine).	Attributed to a combination of factors including intensive training, inappropriate dietary intake and low levels of body fat.	Provide training programmes which are caring and sensitive to the needs of and pressures on young female dancers. Training programmes should include individual monitoring, education and counselling.
Eating disorders - resulting from a concern with appearance and % body fat (e.g. anorexia nervosa, bulimia nervosa).	Pressure put on young dancers because: • appearance is important • low body fat is perceived as an advantage in performance • low weight/body fat is expected or insisted on.	Provide training programmes which: • are aware of risks associated with eating disorders • take steps to treat young performers sensitively • help young people to feel in control of their training • are not overly critical of a young person's physique • provide individual monitoring, education and counselling.

Psychological and Emotional Development

'Intelligent, thinking dancers, of all ages and abilities, will have a realistically positive view of themselves, their capabilities and potential as technicians, artists and as people. Dance is rich in opportunities to promote confidence and learning, to enhance personal and social development. This section highlights some key characteristics of psychological development and their implications for dance teachers.

General

Characteristics	Implications for Dance Teachers
Self-belief is a key factor in influencing an individual's chances of realising their full potential.	Use language carefully. Negative comments and criticisms may provide a challenge for some young people; for many others they may be internalised, 'taken to heart' and limit the individual's potential to achieve.
Negative comments have a greater impact and are more readily believed and remembered than positive ones.	Use encouragement, praise and positive feedback more frequently than negative criticism.
Most people are acutely conscious of their shortcomings, and tend to pay less attention to praise and positive feedback. Destructive 'self-fulfilling beliefs' can be very difficult to change.	Identify global, enduring positives such as "you're really good at", where possible based on evidence to make the praise honest and real.
'Failure' is often ascribed to personal shortcomings, while 'success' may be ascribed to external factors such as luck or chance.	Help students to accept their success. Encourage them to understand, articulate and acknowledge their own role in their achievements.
Children and young people are sensitive to comments and actions that appear to define who they are. Parents, teachers and people who are perceived as having 'authority' or who are significant in their lives play an important role in defining their sense of self and self-worth.	Consider the whole person and treat all students as individuals, emphasising their individual strengths. Aim to give attention to all students equally, being aware of behaviour and body language as well as verbal feedback.
Movement, memory and learning are interrelated. Learning and thinking require the ability to sequence and manipulate information. Physical activity can produce chemical alterations that strengthen the brain, and can improve academic ability, memory retrieval and cognitive development. Physical movements use some of the same brain activity used for reading.	Learning in dance is part of the individual's wider learning experience. Patterns, sequences and repetition can aid the development of language and learning skills. Reflecting on, articulating and discussing experiences enhances learning.

Early Years and Primary School

Characteristics	Implications for Dance Teachers
From around the age of two, children begin to develop their sense of 'self' - who am I and where do I fit in? From a young age children are susceptible to understanding their own worth in relation to the responses and feedback they receive from others.	Positive affirmation promotes the confidence to explore, discover and learn.
Young children perceive and understand the world physically.	Movement, rhythm and music play an important role in early learning, in finding out about the world and communicating with others. Physical exploration and learning underpin the mental processes that promote cognitive development.
Young children see themselves as the centre of their world, and gradually gain understanding of themselves in the context of the wider world.	Consider the social aspects of dance activities. Learning to relate to others, to take turns, to experience being part of a group, develop language etc. can all be fostered through dance activities.
Language develops from an early age and involves forming mental categories, learning vocabulary, developing sentences and the social use of language.	Listen and respond. How much, and how patiently, children will listen is influenced by how their own attempts at communication are received.
Between the ages of five and eight children may not be able to discern 'fact' from opinion or fantasy, especially when expressed by a person of authority or importance in their lives.	Avoid global, enduring negatives, such as "you're clumsy" as children may believe that they apply across all situations.
From around the age of seven children are capable of independent thought, making judgements, appreciating that others have views and developing their own value systems.	Demonstrate respect for their views. It will help give them the confidence to test and review their opinions and encourages them to respect the views of others.
As language develops, children are increasingly able to present arguments, question, give accurate descriptions and information.	Provide opportunities for students to develop their dance language, use appropriate and specific terminology (e.g. anatomical, artistic and choreographic) and to articulate their responses to experiences.
As social skills develop, children are better able to work in pairs and groups.	Provide guided, structured opportunities to work with others. Introduce self-directed tasks gradually, providing opportunities to negotiate, make decisions and take responsibility.

Secondary School

Characteristics

Moving from primary to secondary school marks a significant change in the lives of young people and is a milestone in the progress to adulthood. Physical changes in their bodies also have psychological implications. They may be more emotional and more self-conscious.

Peer pressure becomes more significant and influential – e.g. they may decide to stop dancing because of peer pressure.

Young people develop a clearer sense of their own strengths and weaknesses. This may be informed by extrinsic measures, such as examination results, or more subjective measures, such as how often they are asked to demonstrate, receive feedback, etc.

Young people become increasingly adept at dealing with abstract thought and using a variety of solutions to solve problems.

Implications for Dance Teachers

Treat them as young adults, with choices and other demands on their time. Recognise their wider context.

Being encouraged to feel secure about who they are, their achievements and potential will help them to consider options and make their own decisions.

Provide positive feedback based on reality and concrete examples. Encourage a realistically positive view of themselves, their capabilities and their potential.

Provide the context for what they are doing and why. Challenge them to think as well as to do.

Young Dancers

Characteristics

Aspiring dancers may be highly motivated. In their desire to achieve and succeed, they may lose sight of their strengths.

The emphasis on physical excellence may lead to unrealistic body image and eating disorders.

The ambition and drive to dance may lead to unrealistic expectations of a performing career.

Implications for Dance Teachers

Encourage their development as dancers, artists and as people. Avoid emphasising the dancer at the expense of the artist or the person.

Be aware of the danger signs. Have procedures in place to support young people should the need arise.

Encourage an understanding of the realities of a performing career and consideration of the personal qualities needed. Encourage an understanding of the potential range of dance careers including different kinds of performing and options such as teaching, writing, managing. Encourage wide interests, including continuation of education and obtaining academic qualifications.

Physical Disabilities

Sue Smith

Theses notes are based on experience of working primarily with integrated groups of people with and without physical disabilities and sensory impairments. They reflect thoughts about participating in dance activity primarily as a way of experiencing the creation of dance and the development of movement skills. The value of dance as a therapeutic tool and the range and diversity of activity in this area is acknowledged. Some of the points raised will be relevant across the board. These notes do not intend to reflect practice across all activity in the field of dance and disability.

Photo: Eric Richmond

Choreographers/dancers for **Mission Tour 2001 & 2003**, Robert Hylton and Bawren Tavaziva

Who?
Be clear about who is participating. If there are facilitators/personal assistants, there should be clarity about what their role is. Is it appropriate for assistants to 'help' their clients dance? Or do you want to encourage an individual, autonomous response?

Find out the best way to communicate with each participant. Always address people directly. Never make assumptions about a person's level of understanding. Give each person time to communicate and to establish how this takes place – perhaps through a liberator/descriptor book or assistant. Take the time to wait for a person using an electronic communicator to speak. Some people have an affirmative signal: speak to assistants/key workers if necessary to find out what it is.

Establish that each person is there in their own right – to participate or to observe.

Safety needs addressing early on. Identify issues in the space and emphasise a need to ask questions – either of the teacher/leader or someone else in the group. You won't know everything about everybody's body so be honest about this. Participants should be encouraged to take responsibility for their own bodies. In a group where physicalities are very diverse, it is important to establish that responsibility for safety is shared.

Communication
Ensure effective communication with each participant. Finding the right language is important. Always address the individual you are talking to and only use a facilitator/assistant if you have to. It is important to have the confidence to find the best way to work with each participant and to remain open to new ways. Always ask for advice and guidance from participants and those around you.

There is huge debate about language and disability. What is acceptable for one school/group or person may be offensive to another. You will soon be corrected if a participant is not happy with your terminology. It is not generally seen to be impertinent to ask a person about how best to give instruction or about the extent to which a movement or task can be developed, e.g. "Can you take that further?" or "Try and find a way to do that with a different quality".

Photo: John Cole

Cando2

If you can find this level of communication, it is possible to start to push and challenge individuals. If you appear nervous about how somebody's body moves, it will be difficult to facilitate exploration.

Establishing an openness and willingness to listen will help find the best way to address the group. Be direct and if you are unsure about anything, ask. Never make assumptions about what a person is or will be comfortable with. Putting the emphasis on the individual to communicate issues frankly can steer you away from an inappropriate focus on what a person cannot do.

Intelligent and sensitive use of language can improve a relationship with a group, for example:

- "Ready to move?" instead of "Stand up!"
- "Reach for the ceiling." instead of "Reach your hands up."
- "Move around the space." rather than "Walk around the space."

Openness and honesty encourage effective communication and help to establish respectful relationships.

Starting to move

Even if you know a group/individual well, you should state clearly that you need to share the responsibility of finding the best way to meet the challenge of the work. Identify what your aims are and refer to these rather than their physical representation on a particular body type, i.e. achieving a particular quality or dynamic in the movement.

Be clear that instructions should be applied according to individual physicality. This is a great equaliser. "As fast as you can" will be different speeds for different people. It helps to refer to this shared understanding of instructions to reinforce that you expect individual responses and a shared interpretation of instruction can produce different outcomes.

If it is appropriate, try to develop ways to work which do not rely on groups executing identical sequences or steps. This can be alienating and reinforce barriers.

Demonstration

Demonstration should be varied and relevant to all participants and be able to inspire without alienating. In a group with a diverse physical range, it is important to show how the task can work for all. Again refer to the aims of the task and emphasise the movement principles and intention.

Recognise value across the range of work presented by the group and draw attention not only to different people but also how to build on the quality of their work. Integrated dance should not be about 'joining in' with something able bodied people do. Quality of movement needs to be encouraged, recognised and developed in all participants.

Photo: Kevin Low

Scottish Dance Theatre, *Daddy I'm not Well*

Expectations

Through clarity in the quality of the work you want to achieve and openness in exploring possibilities, students have the opportunity to meet the teacher's and their own expectations and to exceed them. Quality of movement and focus are not determined by body type but by a teacher's ability to offer routes to create and develop movement and to facilitate creativity.

The work delivered should allow individuals to achieve their potential and make progress in the time given.

By identifying the purpose of movement tasks and exercises it is possible to distil the movement principle being used. Deconstructing familiar teaching devices/methods to clarify the aims can be a useful process.

Working with a signer

If participants use British Sign Language (BSL) and there is a signer present:

- Make sure they can see you.
- Don't speak too quickly.
- Be efficient with language and emphasise key points.
- Make your commands visual as well as aural.
- Give the signer regular breaks (about every 45 minutes).

Visual impairment

- Don't make assumptions about the level of impairment.

- Demonstrate tasks with participants if appropriate.
- Do not stand in front of a window to talk or demonstrate.
- Is the venue a known environment?
- Use music sensitively.
- Be aware of emphasis on eye contact.
- You can usually get everyone's attention by flicking the lights on and off.

Reminders

- Each individual participates in their own right.
- Establish the best way to communicate with participants, as a foundation for setting and developing movement ideas and developing interaction.
- Ensure each person is heard.
- Participants should speak on their own behalf to encourage responsibility for reactions, thoughts, feelings.
- Work with participants to understand how tasks may work for them.
- Don't be afraid to ask about the level and nature of impairment – it's important to know.
- Reiterate the importance of asking questions if something isn't clear.
- Participants take responsibility for their own bodies.
- Stay open to finding the best way to work.
- Take time to achieve results – this is a journey.

Learning Difficulties

Sarah Edwards

These notes are based on working with pupils who experience severe learning difficulties, both within a discrete setting and within inclusive groups. There are many well-established groups and practice continues to be exciting in this field. Groups can be found within schools, working as dance companies and on discrete projects. The range of provision is worth exploring prior to embarking on a project, whether that is within the targeted organisation or further afield. A lot can be learnt from sharing the experience.

All individuals

Establishing each participant's individuality is an essential part of getting the practice right. Treat each setting you step into as a new opportunity and make no assumptions about it. The phrase 'learning difficulties' can mean different things to different people, is hard to define and is sometimes transient. You may come across terms such as mild, moderate, special educational needs, autism, challenging behaviour, severe learning difficulties, complex learning difficulties and so on. Sometimes such terms are helpful, but every school, college or youth club is so different that it is probably just as worthwhile finding out about the needs of each individual a little, before you start work. It is always better to see what people can do rather than guess at what they can't.

Other staff

Staff who already work within the group will have a wealth of information about the young person and their capabilities, and, in some situations, so will the individual! This will be a useful starting point as well as your own observations, written information and video footage. Try to have any conversations that refer directly to the individual in private, but also include time in the schedule for group sharing and discussion. Be clear about what you expect from staff supporters and think about setting ground rules for the whole group. For example: Is everyone in kit? Does everyone do a warm up? Do you shape movements through demonstrations and physical prompting? Or through free movements? Build in time for evaluation and feedback, especially in the earlier sessions. Think about whether you want whole group feedback, or a mix and match version where staff get some time and the dance group also meet.

Communication and pace

Find out the preferred mode of communication for the group and for individuals. It may be that you have to use some basic Makaton signs or symbols. Always supplement your spoken instruction. Do not patronise, and continually check that you are being understood. It may be that you need to adapt the complexity of your instructions: try reducing to a single instruction or concept at a time. You may also need to change the pace, adapt your expectations or repeat and revise a lot more than you are used to. Demonstration is an essential part of your repertoire when communicating effectively. Don't forget to demonstrate yourself as well as asking participants and staff to do it.

Process and performance

The process of creating a dance piece has equal value to performing the piece itself. During the process the individual can develop in so many ways – including ways that might not have been planned for. Communication, self-esteem and discipline can all develop during a dance project. This is why it is important to remain flexible, to listen and to give space for individual growth. It is valid to come in with ideas, structure and vision – but without the contributions of the individuals involved these thoughts will be sterile.

Integrating personalised movements into a structure is easy and it begins to give early ownership of the piece to the group. Have high expectations and they will be exceeded; instil discipline into the dancers and they will generalise it; encourage quality of movement and they will teach it to others.

Performing a piece is an important (I would say an essential) part of any dance intervention. (Remember that performing to peers, or in a special sharing evening or to a feeder school is always easier to set up.) At the very least, encourage regular performing to each other within the session. This encourages critical reflection, group creativity and problem-solving. It also begins to shape what being an audience means. Aiming towards an end goal always creates an edge and purpose to rehearsal time and is an excellent motivator. Do not be wary of putting the group under this kind of pressure or scrutiny. I have found that with careful preparation participants respond well to the challenge. It is critical to work on performance qualities from the start of the intervention. Set group rules from the outset that everyone can grasp. For example, no talking during performance (audience, adults, performers), whenever the music is on you need to be in role/dancing. Work with the group on how to look beyond the audience, how to wait off stage. (Establish on and off stage areas, even in the rehearsal space. Establish stage front early on and try to keep this constant.) Do not underestimate the power of preparation. These things will have to be rehearsed as much as the piece itself – but they will come! It is essential to have rehearsed in the space the piece is going to be performed in. Try to have rehearsed using the exact conditions of the performance as far as possible. In my experience last-minute changes - such as a

new costume, make-up, change of lighting or a new piece of scenery - are the things which can throw inexperienced performers.

Music

The ideal is to have access to a live musician, but this is not always possible. So what to choose? It is worth thinking about the possible mood(s) of the dance – does this influence the choice of music?

Experience has shown that though it is possible to find a piece of music which has main movement changes clearly marked, these musical cues may be too subtle for the group. It is therefore sometimes useful to have live percussion over the top of this piece of music to signal key changes, or to integrate live calling into the piece. Both techniques will compensate for variable counting skills and again transfer independence back to the group.

Summary

- Take time initially to find out about the setting and the individuals
- Formulate some ideas but be ready to make adaptations
- Think carefully about being multi-sensory in your presentations
- Build in time for discussion and evaluation.
- Be prepared to adapt the pace and language you are using
- Have high expectations
- Always work on the performance group rules
- Rehearse the performance conditions
- Evaluate

Teachers Self-evaluation Checklist

Class: .... **Date:** ....

Did I?	How well	Notes for next time
Set clear objectives and plan the class	1 2 3	
Prepare resources in advance	1 2 3	
Check the space and adapt my plans accordingly	1 2 3	
Welcome the students, check their names and introduce the objectives for the class	1 2 3	
Ensure everyone was warmed up	1 2 3	
Provide clear instructions, explanations and demonstrations	1 2 3	
Provide appropriate background information	1 2 3	
Relate material and ideas to the wider world of dance	1 2 3	
Check for understanding	1 2 3	
Use positive language and imagery	1 2 3	
Rotate students' places in the room/change my place in the room	1 2 3	
Use a range of teaching resources and strategies	1 2 3	
Maintain a balanced pace to the class	1 2 3	
Give attention to and involve everyone in the class	1 2 3	
Provide positive feedback, praise and encouragement	1 2 3	
Allow sufficient time for students to reflect on and articulate their learning	1 2 3	
Meet the objectives I set for the class	1 2 3	

What did I learn?

Did the class contribute to my longer-term objectives?

General comments and points for future classes:

Watching Dance

Questions to promote observation, reflection, evaluation and discussion.

Cheshire Dance

Observation, physical literacy and learning are encouraged by being given indications of what to look for, looking, and being asked about what has been seen and why conclusions have been reached. What follows is not an exhaustive list of questions, and the questions are not written for a specific age group. They may be helpful to teachers assessing dance technique and choreography, and to young people who wish to develop their observational and critical skills. They may also prompt more questions.

Ideas and overall responses
How did you enjoy the piece? Could you appreciate it and see value in it even if you did not particularly like or enjoy it?

How would you describe your response to the piece? Did you find it enjoyable, intriguing, challenging, magical, difficult, mystifying or moving? What other words describe how you felt?

What do you think the choreographer was aiming to convey?

What was effective about the piece? How effective was the movement vocabulary, structure, use of the space, performance, use of sound, design of the lighting, set and costumes?

What kind of atmosphere or mood did the piece create? What were the characteristics of the atmosphere, how was it created?

What ideas could you see in the piece? How were the ideas conveyed? Did you recognise or empathise with any of the ideas?

How did the piece surprise you? Did it cause you to think differently about anything?

What feelings, thoughts and ideas of your own did the piece spark?

Movement vocabulary
How effective were the movements in expressing the ideas? How would you describe the range of movements used?

Did the movements have a coherent style? What words best describe the style? Could you describe the characteristics and dynamics that gave them their style?

What images did the movements evoke for you? Did they create shapes in space, flow through the dancers bodies seamlessly, surprise, or echo and stylise real life?

How would you describe the relationship between the movement and the music? Did the movements express the music, work in parallel with the music or play with the music?

Photo: Tom Martin

Dance 4

Structures

How would you describe the overall structure, or design of the piece? For example, was it a series of peaks and troughs, a symmetrical curve, or something else?

Was there a narrative to the piece? Did it have different acts or different sections? How did these fit together?

How did the ideas and movements develop? Were sequences repeated, perhaps with different numbers of dancers, different timings or different intentions?

What patterns could you see emerging in the way movements, sequences and dancers worked together? How would you describe the patterns?

Did the piece work within a particular range of dynamics, or use many different dynamics? Could you sense an ebb and flow of energy?

How would you describe the pace of the piece? Was a consistent pace maintained, or were contrasting speeds used?

Did the structure follow the music, or did the dance have a structure of its own?

How did the dancers relate to each other, the space and with the audience?

What movement phrases could you identify? Were there any particularly memorable phrases? What made them memorable?

How did the piece end? Was it a breath-taking climax, a peaceful resolution, a question mark or something else?

Performance

How confident or assured were the dancers in their performance? Did you get a sense that they believed in and were committed to what they were doing?

How did the dancers make sense of the movements, phrases and dance as a whole? Did they illuminate the movement phrases with something of themselves?

How did the dancers work together? Did they support each other and create a sense of group? How would you describe the dancers' relationships with each other?

How effectively did the dancers make use of the space, their energies and focus?

Were the dance and its setting appropriate to each other? Could you imagine the dance in a different setting?

How did the theatrical design features - lighting, sound, costumes, set - contribute to the power of the whole piece?

Risk Assessment

In an increasingly litigious society, a culture of blame becomes common and people become 'risk averse'. No activity is entirely free from risk. Carrying out assessments minimises risks and put them into perspective. The purpose is to anticipate problems in order to reduce the likelihood of accidents or injuries, and to be prepared to deal with any that might occur.

Photo: John McPake

Healthier Dancer Event in Clackmannanshire

Employers may require formal risk assessments to be undertaken. This could include completing forms that need to be checked and signed off by another member of staff. Local authorities and other bodies may require independent teachers to carry out risk assessments for activity taking place on their premises or with their financial support. Completing and recording risk assessments demonstrates that the appropriate care and responsibility has been exercised. A sample risk assessment form is provided at the end of this section.

Activity

Risk assessments are undertaken for a specific activity, such as: going to see or taking part in a performance in a theatre; attending an external examination or audition; or for a series of activities, such as regular classes, a tour of performances or a site-specific performance project. In particular, activities that are new or out of the ordinary will be assessed for risk. This might include a one-off class or workshop.

Risks

The key concern is the health and safety of everyone involved. (Refer to *Safe Practice*). Factors to consider include:

- Nature of the activity: e.g. how familiar everyone is with the activity and location, size of group, age of participants.

- Environment: e.g. hazards such as slippery, weak or solid floors, low ceilings, obstructions, limited wing space, side lighting, camera flashes, the general safety of the site, temperature, noise, weather.
- Use of equipment: e.g. chairs, ladders, tools, electrical equipment, sound or lighting rigs, scenery, breakable equipment, potential injury caused by equipment.

Assessing risk

- Specify the activity.
- Consider the potential risk(s). What might happen?
- Consider the probability of the risk(s). How likely is it? How frequently might it occur?
- Consider the severity of the risk(s). How dangerous might it be?
- Consider the factors that might increase the probability or severity of the risk.

For example: what if a fire broke out in a theatre where you were responsible for a group of young people performing? The likelihood of it happening is small, but the potential danger is great. The probability of it happening would be higher if costumes were made of flammable materials, and the severity of the risk of personal injury would also be higher.

Anticipating and reducing risk
The steps that can be taken:

Know what to expect – The more that is known, the more chance there is of avoiding accidents and injury, e.g. a pre-visit to the site, good briefing of all participants, ensuring everyone knows the location of fire doors and the health and safety rules, clear understanding of what is expected of everyone involved, who to go to if a problem arises.

Forward plan – Think through the detail of what is going to happen, e.g. allow adequate time for briefing and preparation, travel, breaks, getting ready etc., have appropriate insurance and permissions from parents.

Be prepared – Imagine what might happen if.... e.g. have contact phone numbers, a mobile phone, and access to appropriate first aid.

To continue the example of a fire in a theatre, reducing risk would include ensuring:
* everyone, including parent-helpers, knows the layout of the backstage area and where fire doors are located
* everyone knows what to do in the event of fire, who to report it to and how to behave
* you have an accurate list of all the members of the group
* you know how to contact parents or carers should the need arise.

Other risks
For freelance, self-employed or independent teachers, there may be legal, financial or other business risks to consider.

Photo: Niki Sianni

**Dancers-Mothers Project,
Royal Festival Hall Education**

Sample Risk Assessment Form

Activity:	
Location:	Date(s):
Risks assessed by:	

Risk	How probable?	How serious?

Actions taken

Risk	How probable?	How serious?

Actions taken

Risk	How probable?	How serious?

Actions taken

Risk	How probable?	How serious?

Actions taken

Signed: .... Date: ....

Questions Parents Might Ask

How do I find a dance teacher?
Check local papers and the Yellow Pages telephone directory. Dance Agencies usually offer a range of dance opportunities for young people, and may hold directories or know of other opportunities in the area. The teaching organisations have lists and contact details of teachers that offer their examinations.

How do I know if a teacher is good?
Qualifications indicate to parents and learners that a teacher has the essential knowledge, skills and understandings. It is as important that the individual teacher's style suits the individual learner. People learn in different ways, and we all learn best from people we like and respect.

The best teachers will welcome questions, for example, about:
• their experience, qualifications and any organisations that they might be affiliated to
• their approach, teaching objectives and values
• the opportunities they offer, for example, to perform, take examinations, go and see performances, participate in events or festivals, work with visiting teachers and professional artists.

You could also talk to other parents and young people who already attend classes, check on the teacher's local reputation, the physical surroundings in which they teach and watch a class.

Can we go to more than one school?
It will depend on the teacher. Some teachers are reluctant for their students to go to other teachers. While they cannot insist (unless it is a part of the formal rules of the school or a contract with the parents), they may have good reason for their view. Talk to the teacher.

How much will it cost?
Find out about fees. Some teachers offer a discount for paying in advance, or for more than one class or one child. In addition to fees, ask about other costs such as special clothing and shoes, examination fees, etc.

At what age can children start dancing?
Some teachers offer classes for very young children and their parents/carers. Teachers can advise on the appropriate age to start - and it is never too late - although some, usually classical, dance forms take many years of training and experience to reach a professional standard.

What kind of time commitment is involved?
Usually, at least one class a week during term times. Most schools and agencies offer more opportunities. How much time your child should spend dancing will depend on their age, maturity, strength, energy and how much they want to do. Ensure that children and young people are not overloaded, and have adequate time for rest, school work and other activities.

In order to minimise the risk of injury, young people need to prepare for progression to more intensive training, for example when starting a foundation course or full-time training.

What can I do if my child's school does not offer dance?

Talk to the headteacher and find out why. It may be due to pressure on the time-table, lack of suitable space or lack of dance expertise in the teaching staff. It may be possible for the school to start an out-of-hours club, to invite a professional company to provide a dance project, or to work in partnership with other local schools or dance providers. Talk to other parents to find out how much support there might be for dance opportunities.

What can I do if I think my child is talented?

Does your child want to pursue dance as a possible career? Find out about the options available locally and seek lots of advice about which ones might best suit your child's interests and talents. Seek other opinions about your child's talent. If under the age of 11, your child might want to audition for a specialist boarding school. You might want to select a primary or secondary school that has a strong dance department or recognised arts status. Your child might want to consider going on to a vocational training school at 16 or 18, or taking dance at university.

What if my child stops enjoying their dance classes?

Find out why. Has something happened that should be discussed with the teacher? Has the teacher noticed your child has lost interest? Have they reached a point in their growth and/or development when they feel they are not progressing as quickly as they would like? Consider moving to a different teacher or different kind of dance.

Photo: Roy Peters for Peppy Hills

SUNMOVES a land based arts project

Further Information

Contacts

Association of Dance of the African Diaspora
020 7978 7101
www.adad.org.uk

Community Dance Wales – Dawns Gymuned
Cymru
02920 575075
www.communitydancewales.com

Council for Dance Education and Training
020 7247 4030
www.cdet.org.uk

Dance Books
01420 86138
www.dancebooks.co.uk

Dance Teachers Benevolent Fund
C/o Dancing Times
Clerkenwell House
45-47 Clerkenwell Green
London
EC1R 0EB

Dance UK
020 7228 4990
www.danceuk.org

Foundation for Community Dance
0116 251 0516
www.communitydance.org.uk

Healthier Dancer Programme
020 7228 4994
www.danceuk.org

National Dance Teachers Association
www.ndta.org.uk

National Resource Centre for Dance
01483 689316
www.surrey.ac.uk/NRCD

Qualifications and Curriculum Authority
020 7509 5556
www.qca.org.uk

Arts Councils

Arts Council of England
020 7333 0100
www.artscouncil.org.uk

Arts Council of Northern Ireland
02890 385200
www.artscouncil-ni.org

Arts Council of Wales – Cyngor Celfyddydau
Cymru
02920 376500
www.ccc-acw.org.uk

Scottish Arts Council
0131 226 6051
www.sac.org.uk

Teaching organisations

Association of American Dancing
01663 774 986

British Association of Teachers of Dancing
041 423 4029
www.batd.co.uk

British Ballet Organization
020 8748 1241
www.bbo.org.uk

British Theatre Dance Association Head Office
0116 2622279
www.btda.org.uk

Imperial Society of Teachers of Dancing
020 7377 1577
www.istd.org

International Dance Teachers Association
0151 728 7800
www.idta.co.uk

National Association of Teachers of Dancing
01635 868888
www.natd.org.uk

Royal Academy of Dance
020 7223 0091
www.rad.org.uk

Scottish Dance Teachers' Alliance
0141 339 8944

Spanish Dance Society
01784 460419

United Teachers of Dance
0121 373 5883

National Dance Agencies

England

Association of National Dance Agencies (ANDA)
www.anda.org.uk

Dance 4
0115 941 0773
www.dance4.co.uk

Dance City
0191 261 0505
www.dancecity.co.uk

Dance East
01473 639 230
www.danceeast.co.uk

Dance North West
01606 863 845
www.dancenorthwest.org.uk

DanceXchange
0121 622 3253
www.dancexchange.org.uk

The Place
020 7380 1268
www.theplace.org.uk

South East Dance
01273 202 032
www.southeastdance.org.uk

Swindon Dance
01793 463 210
www.swindondance.com

Yorkshire Dance
0113 243 9867
www.yorkshiredance.org.uk

Scotland

Citymoves Dancespace
01224 523705

Dance Base – National Centre for Dance
0131 225 5525
www.dancebase.co.uk

Government Departments

Department for Culture, Media and Sport
020 7211 6000
www.culture.gov.uk

Department for Education and Skills
0870000 2288
www.dfes.gov.uk

Music and Dance Scheme
0870000 2288
www.dfes.gov.uk

Further information on teacher training

Graduate Teacher Training Registry (GTTR)
01242 544 788
www.gttr.ac.uk

Laban Guild for Movement and Dance
01621 850441

Teacher Training Agency
01245 454454
www.teach-tta.gov.uk/teach

Universities and Colleges Admissions Service (UCAS)
01242 227 788
www.ucas.ac.uk

Other useful websites

www.artsmark.org.uk

www.londondance.com

www.humankinetics.com

Really useful books

Benjamin, A. (2002) **Making an Entrance: Theory and Practice for Disabled and Non-Disabled Dancers,** Routledge

Buckroyd, J. (2000) **The Student Dancer: Emotional Aspects of the Teaching and Learning of Dance,** Dance Books Ltd.

Ed. Dyke, S. (1999) **The Dancers' Survival Guide,** Dance UK

Evans, J. & Powell, H. (1996) **Inspirations for Dance and Movement,** (Revised Ed.) Scholastic Ltd.

Gough, M. (1999) **Knowing Dance: A Guide for Creative Teaching,** Dance Books Ltd.

Woolf, F. (2000) **Partnerships for Learning: A Guide to Evaluating Arts Education Projects,** Arts Council of England

(2000) **From Policy to Partnership: Developing the Arts in Schools,** Qualifications and Curriculum Authority/Arts Council of England

**All these books were in print at the time of going to press.
A wider selection may be available through libraries.**

Further reading

Ackroyd, S. (2000) **Perspectives on Continuing Good Practice – A Companion to Leading Dance in the Community,** DanceEast

Armstrong, N. & Welsman, J. (1997) **Young People and Physical Activity,** Oxford University Press

Brinson, P. (1991) **Dance as Education,** RoutledgeFalmer

Brinson, P. & Dick, F. (1996) **Fit to Dance? The report of the national inquiry into dancers' health and injury,** Calouste Gulbenkian Foundation. Available from Dance UK

(2001) **A Practical Guide to Vocational Training in Dance and Drama,** Council for Dance Education and Training/National Council for Drama Training

(2002) **An Applicant's Guide to Auditioning and Interviewing at Dance and Drama Schools,** Council for Dance Education and Training/National Council for Drama Training

Davies, M. (2001) **Helping Children Learn through a Movement Perspective,** (New Ed.) Paul Chapman Publishing

Ed. Dyke, S. (2001) **Your Body Your Risk,** Dance UK

Foley, M. (1998) **Dance Floors,** Dance UK

Franklin, E. (1996) **Dance Imagery for Technique and Performance,** Human Kinetics

Grisogono, V. (1993) **Children and Sport: Fitness, Injuries and Diet,** (Reissue) John Murray

Harris, J. & Elbourn, J. (1997) **Teaching Health Related Exercise at Key Stages 1 and 2,** Human Kinetics

Harris, J. & Elbourn, J. (2001) **Warming Up and Cooling Down,** Human Kinetics

Howse, J. & Hancock, S. (2000) *Dance Technique and Injury Prevention,* (3rd Ed.) A&C Black

Jackson, C., Honey, S., Hillage, J. & Stock, J. (1994) *Careers and Training in Dance and Drama,* Institute for Employment Studies

Jones, C. (1994) *Dance! – Education, Training and Careers,* National Resource Centre for Dance

Joyce, M. (1984) *Dance Technique for Children,* Mayfield Publishing

Koutedakis, Y. & Sharp, C. (1999) *The Fit and Healthy Dancer,* John Wiley & Sons Ltd.

Levete, G. (1993) *No Handicap to Dance,* Souvenir Press Ltd.

Pearson, P. (1998) *Safe and Effective Exercise,* Crowood Press

Penrod, J. & Plastino, J. (1998) *The Dancer Prepares,* (4th Ed.) Mayfield Publishing

Peter, M. (1997) *Making Dance Special,* David Fulton Publishers Ltd.

Preston-Dunlop, V. (1998) *Looking at Dances,* Verve Publishing

Robinson, K. (2001) *All Our Futures: Creativity, Culture & Education,* DCMS/DfES. Available from: www.dfes.gov.uk/naccce

Robinson, K. (2001) *Out of Our Minds: Learning to be Creative,* Capstone Publishing Ltd.

Rowland, T. (1990) *Exercise and Children's Health,* Human Kinetics

Ryan, A.J. & Stephens, R.E. (1997) *The Dancer's Complete Guide to Healthcare,* Dance Books Ltd.

Sharp, C. & Dust, K. (1997) *Artists in Schools,* (New Ed.) National Foundation for Educational Research

Taylor, J. & Taylor, C. (1995) *Psychology of Dance,* Human Kinetics

Videos

NDTA (1998) *Teaching Dance in the Primary School*

YMCA Fitness Industry Training (1995) *Getting It Right* (a video about safe exercise technique)

CD/video/booklet:

BBC *Sportsbank Special*

With contributions from:

Laverne Antrobus
Louise Bardgett
Lewis Bergin
Tracey Brown
Deborah Bull
Clare Buxton
Sue Cowley
Sanjeevini Dutta
Sarah Edwards
Jill Elbourn
Lee Fisher
Charlotte Fraser
Louise Glynn
Gil Graystone
Peppy Hills
Stacie Hooks
Andy Howitt
Alex Kenyon
Isaac Ezra Lee-Baker
Kate Mercer
Judith Palmer
Melanie Pope
Bisakha Sarker
Linda Shipton
Matz Skoog
Sue Smith
Pippa Stock
Richard Thom
Brian Thomas
Chris Thomson
Charlotte Vincent
Lauren Vincent
Heidi Wilson

With special thanks to:

Theresa Beattie
Nikki Braun
Gillian Dale
Samira Dubreuil
Doug Durand
Scilla Dyke
Patricia Eckersley
Jasmine Fitter
Alicia Frost
Bobbie Gargrave
Anu Giri
Di Gooding
Marion Gough
Lynn Horsfield
Darryl Jaffray
Rachel Meech
Fiona Melvin
Jane Mooney
Maggie Morris
Jan Nicol
Philip Perry
Michael Platt
Jane Rally
Jacqueline Rose
Lauren Scholey
Gailene Stock
Cindy Sughrue
Kenneth Tharp
Sharon Took-Zozaya
Melanie Wellman
Anne Went
Jan Williams